Contents

Introduction

I'll never forget the very first window I installed. Some childhood friends and I were building a playhouse, and I had scavenged an old sash from a neighbor's trash can. I spent quite a bit of time meticulously building a tight frame for the window so it would keep out the elements. It was the coolest playhouse in our neighborhood because of its "real" glass window. I was quite proud of it. Sadly, one summer morning I discovered that my pride and joy was broken—the pane was shattered and glass fragments were lying on the ground outside the playhouse. I assumed a jealous member of a "rival" club had pitched a rock through it. The strange thing was that I never found a rock inside the playhouse.

Years later, after I'd learned much about carpentry and how wood moves, the mystery of the broken window was finally unraveled. Since I had made the opening fit the sash exactly, there wasn't any room for the window sash to move when the wood swelled with seasonal humidity. As there was no extra space between the frame and the sash, the resulting force shattered the window. Later I found out that room to move is just one reason a window or door needs to be installed in a rough opening. The extra space also allows you to level and plumb the unit, since most framing isn't exact. The moral of the story here is that there's more to windows and doors than meets the eye. It's important to understand not only how the window or door works, but also how it interacts with the house itself.

In this book, I'll start by taking you through window and door design in Chapter 1. I'll begin by going over the different types of doors to choose from and describe where these doors work best and why. Next, I'll take you through the myriad windows available—everything from wood double-hung windows to casement and jalousie windows. Exploded drawings illustrate the different parts of windows and doors so that you can talk sensibly to a window contractor or specialist to order parts or the units themselves.

In Chapter 2, there's detailed information on the general-purpose and specialty tools you'll need to tackle almost any window or door project. This is followed by descriptions of the various material choices you'll have when selecting windows and doors: wood, metal, vinyl, or one of the many new hybrid or "clad" products available. I'll discuss the different windowpane options (single, double, and triple panes), grille options, and screening choices. Finally, I'll cover

RICK PETERS

GREAT WINDOWS & DOORS

A Step-by-Step Guide

STERLING PUBLISHING CO. INC
NEW YORK

Acknowledgements

Butterick Media Production Staff

Photography: Christopher J. Vendetta
Design: Triad Design Group, Ltd.
Illustrations: Triad Design Group, Ltd.
Copy Editor: Barbara McIntosh Webb
Page Layout: David Joinnides

Indexer: Nan Badgett
Project Director: David Joinnides
President: Art Joinnides
Proofreader: Nicole Pressly

Special thanks to Kathy Ziprick with Weathershield for supplying illustrations of glass pane and grille options and for numerous photos throughout; to Linda Mourtinsen with Jen-Weld (Nordco) for the cross section of the double-hung window shown on page 22; to Terry Rex at BFRich for the cross section of the vinyl window on page 23; and to Pozzi Wood Windows for supplying the cross section of a wood window on page 22.
Also, thanks to the production staff at Butterick Media for their continuing support. And finally, a heartfelt thanks to my constant inspiration: Cheryl, Lynne, Will, and Beth. **R. P.**

Every effort has been made to ensure that all the information in this book is accurate. However, due to differing conditions, tools, and individual skill, the publisher cannot be responsible for any injuries, losses, or other damages which may result from the use of information in this book.

Library of Congress Cataloging-in-Publication Data

Published by Sterling Publishing Company, Inc.
387 Park Avenue South, New York, N.Y. 10016
© 2001 Butterick Company, Inc., Rick Peters
Distributed in Canada by Sterling Publishing
c/o Canadian Manda Group
One Atlantic Avenue, Suite 105, Toronto,
Ontario, Canada M6K 3E7
Distributed in Great Britain and
Europe by Cassell PLC
Wellington House, 125 Strand, London
WC2R 0BB, England
Distributed in Australia by Capricorn Link
(Australia) Pty. Ltd.
P.O. Box 6651, Baulkham Hills, Business Centre,
NSW 2153, Australia

Printed in Hong Kong

10 9 8 7 6 5 4 3 2 1

Sterling ISBN 0–8069–5603–8

fasteners used for installation, locksets, weather-stripping, and the best types of caulk recommended for windows and doors.

Chapter 3 delves into the important task of framing openings for doors and windows—everything from types of framing and basic wall construction to using temporary supports. There are also details on how to size headers and install jambs, and step-by-step instructions on how to frame a rough opening. Chapter 4 is all about windows: how to remove a window, install a replacement window, even add a glass block window. There are also instructions on how to install new combination storms, install shutters, and add trim and weatherstripping.

In Chapter 5, I'll take you through some of the most common door projects, like installing a new interior or exterior door, adding a bi-fold door, and—for the more ambitious—installing a sliding patio door where there was no door previously. Other projects include adding a new storm door, attaching trim, installing a replacement threshold, and adding weatherstripping.

The subject of Chapter 6 is installing door and window hardware: sash locks, locksets, security bolts, latches, and door closers. Finally, Chapter 7 takes you through common window and door maintenance and repairs: how to free a stuck window, adjust tension of spiral balances, replace or repair damaged windows and screens, repair a broken window, and so on.

All in all, I hope that this book encourages you to take on a window project or door project that you've hesitated to tackle in the past. Altering a wall, adding a door or window, or upgrading your windows can have a profound impact on your living spaces. I hope that *Great Windows & Doors* helps you with your home improvement adventures.

Rick Peters
Spring 2001

Chapter 1
Window and Door Design

How often have you driven past a home and thought, "Wow, what a great-looking house!" Often, what sets apart a plain, ordinary house from one that's interesting and unique is its windows and doors. The ironic thing is that we often overlook them—if they were chosen to blend in well with the décor, they will add a distinctive or elegant touch without being obvious. The difference between plain windows and those with divided lights can be subtle but will have a large impact on the overall impression of a home.

If your home is looking tired, you're after a new look, or it's simply time to replace outdated windows and doors, the first thing to do is gather information on the choices available. If there's one thing I would stress here, it's don't be satisfied with what's at the local building center. What they carry in stock is only the tip of the iceberg. There are dozens of quality window and door manufacturers (*see the chart at right*), each producing hundreds of products in a wide variety of shapes, sizes, materials, finishes, and colors.

In this chapter, I'll start by explaining the types of doors to choose from:

interior and bi-fold (*opposite page*), exterior and sliding (*page 8*), and swinging and storm (*page 9*). Next, I'll go over the wide variety of windows available: single-hung and double-hung (*page 10*), casement and jalousie (*page 11*), awning and bay (*page 12*), and bow and decorative (*page 13*). Finally, I'll describe the parts of a door (*page 14*) and parts of a window (*page 16*) so that you can discuss windows and doors with confidence with a store clerk or window contractor.

Window and door manufacturers

Manufacturer	Where to get information on the Web
Andersen Windows and Patio Doors	www.andersenwindows.com
BFRich Vinyl Windows and Patio Doors	www.bfrich.com
Pella Windows and Doors	www.pella.com
Pozzi Wood Windows	www.pozzi.com
Stanley Entry Doors	www.stanleyworks.com
Weathershield Wood Windows and Doors	www.weathershield.com
Various manufacturers, including:	**www.doors-windows.com**
Alterna Doors	
Caradco Windows	
Doorcraft Interior Doors	
IWP Doors	
Morgan Doors	
Norco Windows and Patio Doors	
Summit Windows and Patio Doors	
Wenco Windows and Patio Doors	
Willmar Windows	
Yakima Bi-Fold and Café Doors	

Types of Doors

Interior door Interior doors range from simple to decorative. The most common type of interior door is a flush door made up of a wood frame covered with a plywood or solid wood veneer—typically in oak, birch, or lauan. The core of the door can be solid wood, particleboard, or hollow. The term hollow-core door is a bit deceptive: The core isn't technically empty. Instead, it's filled with strips of corrugated cardboard, or other nonwood material, on edge that are then glued to the outer layers, or "skins." This helps support the skins and prevents them from bowing in and incurring damage easily.

More decorative doors, like the one *shown here,* are constructed with a wood frame that holds "floating" panels that can expand and contract with changes in humidity without affecting the door's dimensions.

Bi-fold door A bi-fold door is made up of multiple sections that are hinged together. The hinged portions fold into themselves and slide along a track mounted to the head jamb. Larger door openings can be filled with two sets comprised of four door sections—two folding to the right, and two folding to the left.

Small metal, wood, or plastic pins are installed at the top and bottom of the door sections that butt up against the frame. The top pin fits into a hole in the track, and the bottom pin slips into an L-shaped bracket that's attached to the floor. Bi-fold doors with louvers are popular, as they offer plenty of ventilation—these are particularly useful for closet and laundry-room doors, where clothes are stored. Bi-fold doors are available with solid panels, glass panels, louvered panels, or a combination of these.

Exterior Door Of all the types of doors you can buy, exterior doors come in the greatest variety. That's because many homeowners want to make a personal statement with their front or entrance door—they want a door that's unique, like they are. Hence the huge variety available. Exterior doors are typically constructed out of solid wood or out of metal that's filled with insulation.

Solid-wood doors offer natural beauty and can be easily stained or painted to suit your tastes. Metal insulated doors offer better insulation properties than a solid-wood door, they won't expand and contract with seasonal changes in humidity, and they are considerably tougher than wood doors. A popular style of exterior door, particularly for back doors, is the crossbuck door *shown here*. It features diagonal rails on the lower half and a glass/screened panel on top.

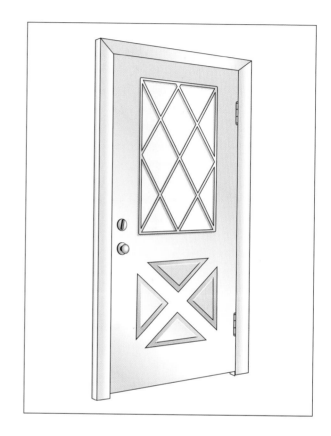

Sliding Door The sliding door has become the door of choice for many homeowners who have a deck. Its large glass sections provide unrestricted viewing, and one or both of the panels slide open to provide excellent ventilation as well as easy access to a deck or porch.

The frames and panels of sliding doors can be made of solid wood, aluminum, or vinyl (like the one *shown here*). In most cases, only one of the panels slides; more expensive sliding doors are available where both panels slide.

Swinging Door Swinging doors are basically two standard doors built into a single jamb. One door is hinged for left-handed operation, and the other door is hinged right-handed. Many homeowners are choosing swinging doors over sliding doors for access to their patio or deck because both doors swing open for maximum ventilation—unlike most sliding patio doors, where only one slides open.

Swinging doors are manufactured in a variety of styles, and one of the most popular styles features divided light panels similar to a French door; *see the drawing at left.* In addition to providing access to a patio or deck, swinging doors can also be used to add privacy to a room. For example, swinging doors can be installed in the opening between a dining room and living room so that either room can be closed off as desired.

Storm Door Storm doors are installed over exterior doors to protect the exterior door and add an additional layer of insulation by creating a sealed airspace between the storm and exterior doors. Most storm doors feature metal frames and house glass panes or screens or both (*see the drawing at left*). One feature to look for in a storm door is self-storing screens—that is, the screen/storm system works much like a storm window, where the screen and storm panels are stored within the frame.

Most storm doors are designed for either right-handed or left-handed installation—you control which way the door opens as you install the metal frame of the door. As with exterior doors, there is quite a variety of styles and finishes to choose from. Full-view storms are popular for entrance doors because they don't obscure the entrance door.

Types of Windows

Single-Hung In terms of appearance, there's little difference between a single-hung and a double-hung window. What is different is whether both the upper and lower sashes have the ability to move. On a single-hung window, only the lower sash can be raised or lowered. With the double-hung window, both sashes can move. This movement also applies to tilting sash windows, like those *shown here:* Only the lower sash on a single-hung window tilts in for easy cleaning.

With this in mind, I always recommend going with a double-hung window. Sure, it may cost a bit more, but the added convenience of being able to clean both sashes by simply tilting them in is worth the extra money. If you are buying windows on a shoestring budget, consider buying single-hung windows for the ground-level windows and double-hung for second-story windows.

Double-hung Both sashes on a double-hung window can be raised or lowered independently of each other. On older windows, the weight of the sash is counterbalanced by sash weights suspended on sash cords. The weights move up and down inside a cavity next to the side jambs. Because this system is bulky and prone to problems, it has been replaced over the years with either a spiral balance (basically an adjustable spring) or a block-and-tackle balance, which operates much like a retractable tape measure. New double-hung windows employ tilting mechanisms that allow for easy cleaning. On many of these, the sashes run in tracks that don't require a parting stop. The space saved is often delegated to thicker sashes that hold double or triple insulating panes (*see page 26 for more on this*).

Casement A casement window is any window where the sash is hinged on the side to allow the sash to pivot in and out like a door. The sash is controlled by way of a scissors-type mechanism, called a casement mechanism, that's operated by turning a crank on the interior of the window.

Most casement windows project outward and therefore provide significantly better ventilation than sliding windows of equal size. That's because the sash projects out from the wall and can be adjusted to catch a breeze. Because of this, screens must be placed on the interior side of the window. Another reason casement windows provide better ventilation over a sliding window is that virtually the entire window can be opened. On sliding windows, only one-half of the available window space can be open at any given time.

Jalousie Jalousie windows are most often found in temperate climates since they offer virtually no insulating properties at all and are almost impossible to seal. Jalousie windows consist of a metal frame that holds strips of glass or louvers. These louvers are connected together so that they open and close simultaneously when a crank or turn-screw is operated inside the window.

The biggest advantage to jalousie windows is ventilation. A wall of these windows can be opened to let in breezes to the point that the inside will feel as if you were outside. This, as I mentioned, is also their largest drawback—when closed, each glass louver rests on the one below, making an airtight seal an impossibility. In addition to this, jalousie windows are a security risk, since all you need to do is bend up the metal tabs that hold a louver in place to remove it and gain access.

Awning Awning windows are hinged at the top and swing open at the bottom. Just like casement windows, awning windows provide greater ventilation over sliding windows, as practically the entire window are can be opened to catch a breeze. Awning windows can be installed so that the sash opens outward (such as in a garage or workshop), or inward in the case of a basement window.

Combination awning windows are available where one or more fixed sashes are combined with one or more operable sashes. Screens and/or storm sashes are optional on most awning windows. One advantage of the way that an awning window opens is that it can usually be left slightly open to provide ventilation even when it's raining.

Bay A bay window protrudes out from an exterior wall to make a room feel larger without the need for expensive structural changes. They are typically made up of three or more windows that project out from the house at a set angle, typically 30, 45, or 90 degrees. The center section is usually parallel with the exterior wall and is made up of one or two units. Each of the window units can be fixed, operating, or a combination of both.

Since bay window units are fairly heavy, care must be taken to fully support the unit during and after installation. Because of this, I generally recommend having a bay window installed by a professional window contractor.

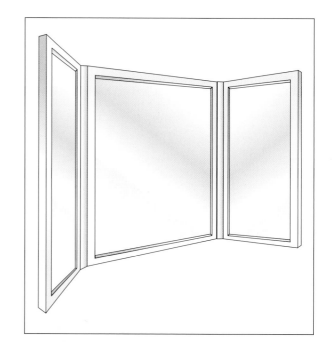

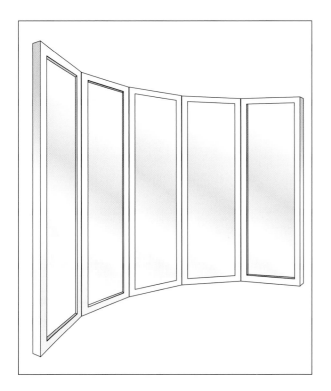

Bow Bow windows are often confused with bay windows, as they appear somewhat similar. The main difference between the two is that a bow window usually has four or five sections that are formed into a graceful curve or bow. Choosing between a bay and a bow window is really a matter of aesthetics: Which do you think will look better on the exterior of the house—the angular look of a bay window, or the flowing curve of a bow window? It's really a matter of personal preference.

Like the bay window, the sections of a bow window may be fixed, operating, or a combination of both. Bow windows are also heavy and need to be supported properly. Here again, I'd recommend professional installation.

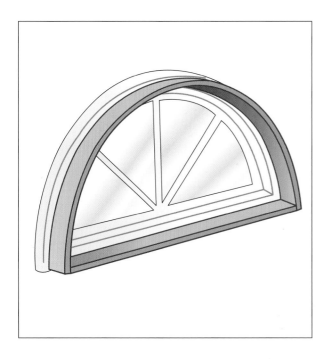

Decorative The variety of decorative window styles, shapes, and sizes available is staggering. Common shapes are: octagon, triangle, trapezoid, pentagon with a flat top, pentagon, hexagon with a flat top, quarter circle, half circle (*shown here*), oval, half ellipse, half cloverleaf, gothic arch, arch top, and full circle—just to name a few.

Because of their unique shape, most decorative windows are fixed, though some are operating. Few home centers stock decorative windows; you'll likely need to find a window contractor or distributor to see what's available and order the windows you want. Note: If you can't find the window of your dreams, most window manufacturers offer custom windows—but be aware that they're not inexpensive.

Door Anatomy

Regardless of the style of the door you choose, all doors share common parts. Framing the door itself are the door jambs: a header and two side jambs. Quite often the side jambs are referred to according to the hardware that attaches to them. The door hinges are mounted to the hinge jamb, and the latch for the lockset is affixed to the latch jamb. The jamb slips into the rough opening for the door and is adjusted for level and plumb with carpenter's shims. When set, the jamb is secured to the framing members by nails driven through the jambs and the shims.

The gap between the jamb and the wall covering is concealed with trim or casing. Trim attached to the outside of an exterior door is typically referred to as brick molding. Trim installed on the interior, or on interior doors, is usually called case molding. In each case, it's attached to the jamb and framing members with long finish nails referred to as casing nails. A threshold, usually metal (but occasionally wood), runs between the jambs at the bottom and covers the gap between the sill and the flooring (most interior doors do not require a threshold). The door itself may be made of solid wood with raised panels (*as shown here*), be made of metal with an insulated core,

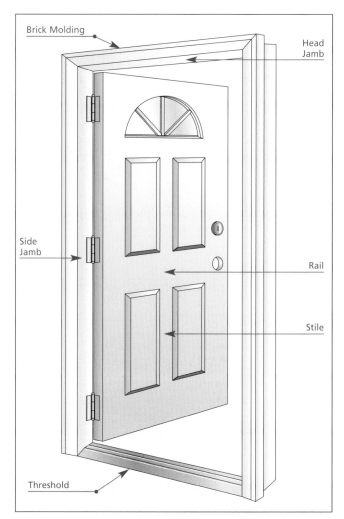

or have a hollow core. Almost every door manufactured is available in either right-handed or left-handed models; *see the sidebar below.*

HANDEDNESS OF DOORS

Here's how to tell whether you want a right-handed or a left-handed door. For doors that swing in, look at the door from the outside of the home. If the hinges are on the left side, it's a left-handed swing-in door; if on the right, it's a right-handed swing-in door. If the door swings toward you, looking at it from the outside of the home, and the hinges are on the left side, it's a left-handed swing-out door; if on the right, it's a right-handed swing-out door.

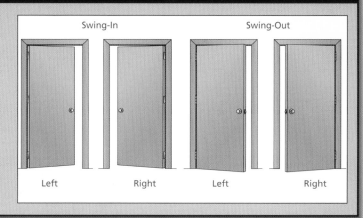

Common door terms

Bi-fold door – a segmented, hinged door that slides on an overhead track and folds into itself.

Café door – a single or double door hung in the middle of a doorway that swings in and out for entry.

Casing – pieces of wood that are surfaced or molded on all four sides, used to trim door openings.

Combination door – a door where the bottom half is wood and the top half is a screen; also called a ventilating door.

Composite door panel – a door panel made of material other than solid wood.

Core – the center portion of a door; it may be solid wood, particleboard, filled with insulation, or hollow.

Crossbuck – a type of door where the panels are separated by diagonal rails.

Decorative entry system – an entryway consisting of a framed door, one or two sidelights, and a transom.

Door frame – the wood parts that are assembled to form the door enclosure.

Doorjamb – the part of a door frame that surrounds and contacts the edges of the door.

Door skin – a panel (typically wood veneer) that forms the face of a flush door.

Door trim – wood molding that's used to finish or "trim" the side of a door frame.

Entrance door – the door in the front or main entrance of a home.

Exterior casing – an exterior casing that serves as the boundary molding for the siding—often referred to as brick molding

Fire-rated door – a door that's rated as to how long it will take to burn; often required between a home and an attached garage.

Flush door – any door that's made up of a core, cross-banding, and flat face veneers.

French door – a door consisting of a top and bottom rail divided by glass panels.

Hollow-core door – a flush door that uses strips of cardboard or other material on edge to support the face veneers.

Kick plate – a thin, metal plate attached to the bottom of a door to protect it from dents, scratches, and dirt.

Panel door – a door made up of panels that fit in a frame consisting of stiles and rails.

Patio door – a door that opens onto a patio or deck; usually made of glass for unobstructed viewing.

Rail – a cross or horizontal portion of a frame.

Raised door panel – a door panel where the edges are shaped to give the panel the appearance of being "raised" above the frame.

Sash door – a door with the bottom half made of wood and the top made of glass.

Sidelight – an assembly of stiles and rails and glass panels that are attached to one or both sides of an exterior door.

Sill – the main horizontal member forming the bottom of the door frame.

Sliding door – a door that opens and closes by sliding one or both panels along a horizontal track.

Stile – the upright or vertical parts of a door.

Storm door – any door that covers and protects an exterior door.

Threshold – a wood or metal strip attached to the bottom of a door to cover the gap between the sill and the floor.

Transom – a top- or bottom-hinged window often found above a door for ventilation.

Window Anatomy

For the most part, windows, with their numerous moving parts, are more complicated than doors. Of all the various types, double-hung windows are the most complex; *see the drawing at right.*

But regardless of the type, all windows have some similar parts. First, they all have one or more panes. These can feature single, double, or triple glazing and may be fixed (nonmovable) or operating (able to open and close). The frame that encases the panes in an operating window is called the sash. The panes within the sash may or may not be divided into smaller panes. The sash travels up and down along the side jambs and is typically held in place with stops and a parting strip.

The base of the window is referred to as the stool. It rests on the windowsill and projects out into the room. A decorative trim piece, called an apron, may or may not be installed directly under the stool.

As with doors, trim or casing is attached to the jamb and to surrounding framing members to conceal the gap between the jamb and the wall covering. Awning and casement windows are hinged on one jamb and open at the bottom and side, respectively. On sliding windows, the sash slides horizontally along a track or set of tracks.

The sash is held open or closed via some type of counterbalance that's inset in the side jambs. Older double-hung windows use heavy cast-iron sash weights. Newer double-hungs utilize some type of spring—either a spiral balance or a block-and-tackle balance.

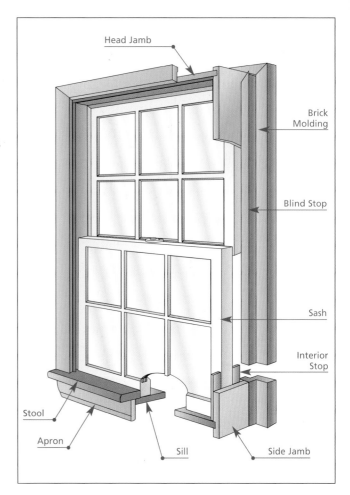

Head Jamb

Brick Molding

Blind Stop

Sash

Interior Stop

Stool

Apron

Sill

Side Jamb

Photo courtesy of Weathershield, © 2001

Common window terms

Aluminum-clad window – a wood window where the exposed parts are covered or clad with aluminum.

Apron – a horizontal trim piece that fits under the sill.

Awning window – a type of window that is hinged on the top and swings open on the bottom.

Balance spring – a device that's used to counterbalance a sash; found in newer double-hung windows.

Bay window – a window that projects out from a wall, typically made up of three glass panels joined at an angle.

Bow window – a rounded bay window that projects from a wall in a graceful arc.

Brick molding – milled wood trim piece that covers the gap between a window frame and the exterior wall or covering.

Casement window – a window that's hinged on the side and that opens and closes via a device called a casement mechanism.

Casing – wood trim attached to the door jamb to cover the gap between the jamb and the wall covering.

Combination window – a window assembly consisting of a half screen and two glass storm panels.

Double glazing – two panes of glass separated by an insulating air space which is often filled with gas to enhance the insulating properties.

Double-hung window – a window where both the top and bottom sash can be moved.

Drip cap – a horizontal molding used to divert water from the top casing.

Fenestration – the placement or arrangement and sizing of windows in a home.

Glazing – the installation of glass in a window opening.

Head jamb – all of the horizontal members at the top of a window frame.

Insulating glass – double- or triple-glazed glass with an enclosed, dehydrated, and sealed space between the panes.

Jalousie – a type of window that's made up of glass slats that pivot open and closed.

Jamb – a vertical member at the side of a window frame.

Mullion – a vertical member between window units.

Muntin – a secondary framing member that's used to hold the window panes in a sash.

Parting strip – a thin wood strip that separates the upper sash from the lower sash into two channels so they can slide up and down independently.

Rail – any horizontal member of a window sash.

Replacement window – typically a double-hung window that's bought as a kit to replace a window without disturbing the interior or exterior walls.

Sash – a framework of rails and stiles that holds the panes of a window.

Sill – the horizontal member at the bottom of a window frame.

Single-hung window – a window similar to a double-hung, where only the bottom sash moves up and down.

Stool – the piece of window trim that provides a stop for the lower sash and extends the sill into the room.

Stop – a narrow strip of wood attached to the head and side jambs to keep the sash in line.

Transom – a horizontal member separating one window panel from another.

Chapter 2
Tools and Materials

Outside of choosing a window or door to replace an old unit or install a new one, selecting and gathering the other tools and materials you'll need for repair, replacement, or new installation work is fairly straightforward. The biggest challenge is choosing the window or door itself. Though most home centers stock some standard-sized doors and windows, you'll often be faced with ordering the size and style you need.

If this is the case, I heartily recommend visiting with a professional window contractor. In many cases, windows and doors are all that these folks deal in—and they know them inside and out. If you need advice on the proper type, size, and style, they can help. You'll be much better off getting advice from them than from a retail clerk at a home center who may have been flipping burgers the week before. Since windows in particular are available in so many sizes, window manufacturers can't afford to stock every size. Instead, they don't make the windows until they receive an order from a contractor. Because this process can take weeks, even months, it's important that they're ordered correctly the first time.

In this chapter, I'll start by going over general-purpose tools you'll want to have on hand in order to tackle most window and door work (pages 19–20). Then I'll identify the few specialty tools that will make your installation and repair work easier (page 21).

Next, I'll help you wade through the myriad choices available for windows—everything from wood and metal to vinyl (pages 22–23). After that, we'll look at choices in doors, including solid-wood, metal, and hollow-core varieties (pages 24–25). In addition to understanding material choices for windows, it's also important to be aware of the different types of panes and screens that are available: single, double, and triple panes—even panes that are filled with gas to enhance the insulation qualities of the window (pages 26–27). Screen options such as fiberglass and aluminum are discussed, along with hints on which type is best for you.

Hardware and weatherstripping choices are also covered in detail, including which type of fasteners are best (page 28), options for locksets (page 29), types of weatherstripping (page 30), and finally, which caulk is best to use for a variety of window and door applications (page 31).

General-Purpose Tools

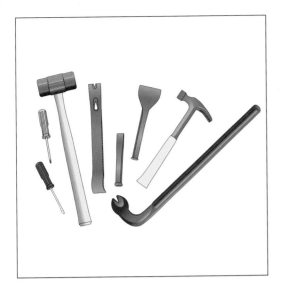

Demolition Many of the window and door jobs you'll tackle will require some demolition work—removing wall coverings or even a section of a wall. You'll find the following tools useful (*from left to right*): screwdrivers for general dismantling, a sledgehammer for persuading stubborn walls to come down, a pry bar for pulling out boards and fixtures, a cold chisel or set of inexpensive chisels for chopping out holes in walls or flooring, a claw hammer for general removal, and a cat's paw for removing nails flush with or below the surface of a workpiece.

Measuring One of the most critical steps in any window or door installation is measuring the openings. The tools *shown* should be in every homeowner's toolbox: a 25-foot tape measure; a framing square to check for perfect right angles; a folding rule for short, accurate measurements; a combination square to check for right angles; and a speed square to take quick, short measurements.

Layout In addition to measuring, laying out intended work is critical to the success of any window or door installation you take on. The following tools should also be in your toolbox: a 4-foot-long level and a shorter torpedo level for checking framing members for level and plumb; a compass to draw circles and arcs; a contour gauge for laying out odd shapes; a plumb bob and string for transferring location points for vertical framing members (such as from ceiling to floor); and a chalk line for striking long layout lines.

Cutting Tools Framing openings requires only a couple of specialized tools for cutting. Although you can cut dimension lumber and trim with a handsaw, it'll be a long day (or days, most likely). If you don't own a power miter saw, or "chop" saw, consider renting one or borrowing one from a friend. In addition to this, you'll need a wood chisel and a block plane for fine-tuning the fit of parts, a compass saw for cutting notches in framing members; a pocket knife or utility knife to trim shims, etc.; and a drywall saw for fitting drywall.

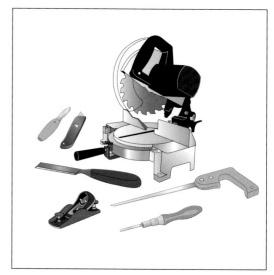

Power tools Power tools can make quick work of many of the tedious tasks associated with installing windows and doors. *Clockwise from top left:* a cordless trim saw for straight-square cuts; a saber saw for cutting access holes; a cordless drill with a ⅜" chuck for smaller-diameter holes; an electric drill with a ½" chuck for larger-diameter holes; a right-angle drill for tight spots; and a reciprocating saw for demolition work.

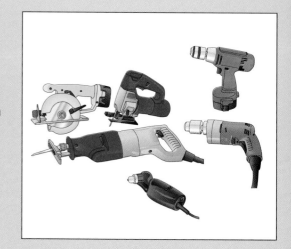

Safety gear As with any home improvement work, it's important to protect yourself by wearing appropriate protective gear. Keep the following on hand (*clockwise from bottom left*): leather gloves to protect your hands; safety goggles to protect your eyes; knee pads not only to cushion your knees, but also to protect them; ear muffs or plugs for when working with power tools; and a dust mask or respirator to protect your lungs from sawdust and the dust raised during demolition.

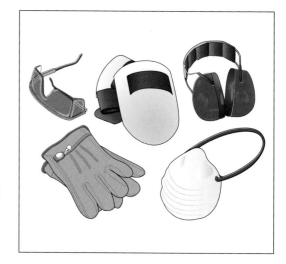

Specialty Tools

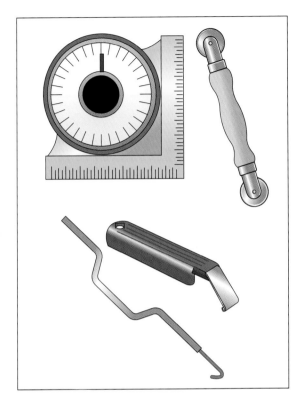

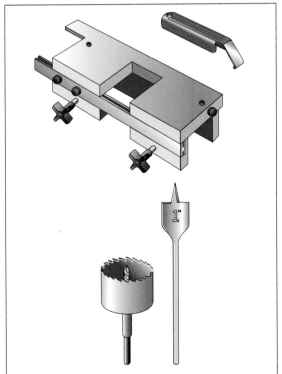

Window tools A common specialty tool for windows is a splining tool (*top right in drawing*). It resembles a double-ended pizza cutter and is used to force rubber spline into the groove in screens to hold the screening in place. One end of the tool is concave to conform to the round spline so it's easy to push the spline in the groove; the other end is convex and is used to preform aluminum screening to make installing the spline easier.

If the double- or single-hung windows in your home use a spiral balance to raise and lower the sash (typically identified by a round tube running the length of the sash), you'll want to purchase a spiral balance adjusting tool (*bottom left in drawing*) so you can adjust the tension of the springs. A sill level (*top left in drawing*) is useful for measuring the angle of the sill—an important step in ordering replacement windows. And if you're working on an exterior window and your home has vinyl siding, you'll want to have a siding-removal tool handy (*bottom right in drawing*).

Door tools If you're installing a prehung door that has the holes for the lockset prebored, you won't need any specialty tools at all. If on the other hand the door is not prehung and the lockset isn't prebored, there are a couple of specialty tools that can help. For doors that aren't prehung, you'll need to cut mortises in the edge of the door to accept the hinges. Here's where a mortising jig like (*top left in drawing*) comes in handy. This type of jig is designed for use with a router and, once set up, will cut extremely accurate mortises.

If the door you're installing doesn't have holes prebored for the lockset, or if you're installing a deadbolt, you'll find a lockset installation kit helpful (*bottom half of drawing*). These kits come in various sizes (to match the varying diameters of locksets) and include a hole saw for the body of the lockset and a spade bit to drill the holes for the latch. Just as with windows, if you're working on an exterior door and your home has vinyl siding, you'll want to have a siding-removal tool handy.

Windows

Double-hung A double-hung window, like the one *shown in the photo at right,* is the most common type of window installed in residential homes. Unlike a single-hung window, where only one sash can be raised and lowered, both sashes on a double-hung window move. Both the upper sash and lower sash encase and protect a windowpane—in this case a double pane. The system *shown* uses a counterbalanced block-and-tackle balance system that allows either sash to be raised or lowered with a touch. Weatherstripping is built in at the head jamb and the check and bottom rails to create a weathertight seal.

Clad The double-hung window *shown here* is the next generation of windows: It features the strength of solid wood, but it's clad with maintenance-free aluminum—typically available in a wide choice of colors (Wood windows are also available clad in vinyl; *see page 23.*) Screens are often an integral part of the system so it's unnecessary to install combination storms to handle the varying needs of the seasons. Most new double-hung windows have numerous options available, such as simulated divided lights or grilles (*see page 27*), and come in a dizzying array of styles and sizes. Consult a local window contractor for more information on styles and choices.

Solid-wood Solid-wood windows are still a good choice, especially when they're well made, like the window *shown at bottom right.* This window is manufactured using high-grade pressure-treated Western pine. Solid-wood windows are less expensive than clad windows and, if cared for properly, will last decades. One big advantage solid-wood windows offer over clad windows is that wood windows readily accept paint—clad windows don't. If you don't care for the color options offered by clad window manufacturers, a solid-wood window is the way to go.

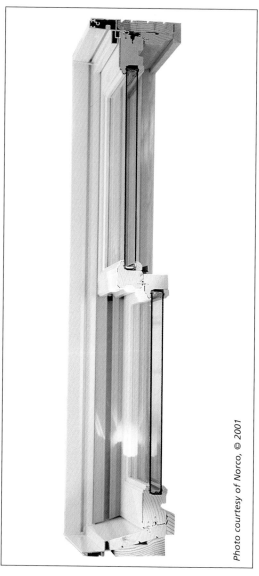

Photo courtesy of Norco, © 2001

Photo courtesy of Pozzi Wood Windows, © 2001

Photo courtesy of BFRich, © 2001

Vinyl Solid-vinyl windows offer a number of advantages over solid-wood and clad windows. They're generally inexpensive and readily available as stock items at most home centers, in a wide variety of sizes. They offer maintenance-free interiors and exteriors, and they don't expand and contract like a wood sash does. Plus they won't chip, peel, or decay over time. As with the other types of windows, solid-vinyl windows offer grille and screen options.

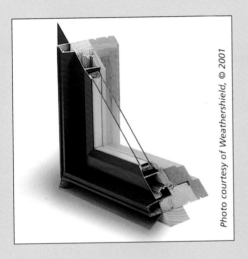

Photo courtesy of Weathershield, © 2001

Hybrid Another window option that offers the best of wood sash and a maintenance-free exterior is a hybrid window, like the one *shown here.* This type of window features wood parts but has an exterior that's all metal—in this case, aluminum. Various styles of brick molding are available for the exterior metal section, along with numerous color choices. Contact your local window contractor for sizes and colors that can be ordered.

CLEANING TILTING-SASH WINDOWS

One of the most convenient features of the new generation style of tilting-sash windows is how easy they are to clean; *see the photo at right.* Simply depress both sash releases at the top or bottom of the sash, and tilt the window down so that you can clean the exterior side. Tilt the sash back into place after cleaning, reset the releases, and move on to the next sash—no more climbing on ladders or stepstools. What a timesaver, especially for second-story windows!

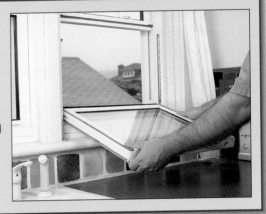

Doors

Shopping for a new door—particularly a new front door—can be a mind-numbing experience. That's because there are numerous materials, dozens of styles, and thousands of doors to choose from. Start by deciding what type of door material will work best for you. The two most common choices are solid wood and metal. Solid-wood doors offer natural beauty and can be stained or painted to fit your décor. Metal doors can also be painted, and they offer stability, strength, and good insulating properties. If you're planning on painting the door, I'd recommend a metal door; for a natural look, go with solid wood (or check out the new metal doors that have an outer skin of wood veneer). If you're replacing a door or are installing a new one and the rough opening is a standard dimension, go with a prehung door—they're just so much easier to install. Regardless of the type you choose, look for quality construction and as high an insulation value as you can find (here's where metal-insulated doors really shine).

Solid-wood A door made of solid wood is still a common choice for many homeowners. That's because the natural beauty and strength of wood is a welcoming touch to any home. Most solid-wood doors feature mortise-and-tenon construction and have raised panels that "float" in grooves in the door frame. This allows the panels to move with seasonal changes in humidity without causing the door to bind. (Note: Even the best-made door will swell in the summer and shrink a bit in the winter.)

Metal Metal doors have a number of advantages over solid-wood doors. First, since they're metal, they won't swell or contract with seasonal changes in humidity like a wood door does. Second, the hollow core of the door can be filled with foam to provide insulation. Third, metal doors are tough—they stand up extremely well to regular use (and abuse). Metal doors are available in a multitude of shapes and sizes and can even be found covered with a wood veneer to give the appearance of solid wood.

Hollow-core Hollow-core doors are designed for interior use since they're not heavy-duty enough, nor do they offer the insulating properties that solid-wood or metal doors do. Hollow-core doors are made by covering a wood frame with two sheets or "skins" of wood veneer, typically lauan, birch, or oak. Although you'd assume the core (the space between the skins) is empty, it's not. Instead, there are strips of corrugated cardboard on edge, glued to the skins in an X pattern. This does a surprisingly good job of supporting the skins, preventing them from bowing in.

PREHUNG DOORS VS. STANDARD

Whenever it comes to installing a new door, I always recommend using a prehung door (*left drawing*)—it's just a whole lot easier. There are no mortises to cut, no hinges to install, no holes to drill. All you need to do is slip it into the rough opening, shim it so it's plumb and level, and nail it to the framing members. If it's so easy, why would you ever want to install a standard door (*right drawing*)? Standard doors are useful for odd-sized doors that need to be trimmed to fit and for when you just can't find the style of door you're looking for in a prehung.

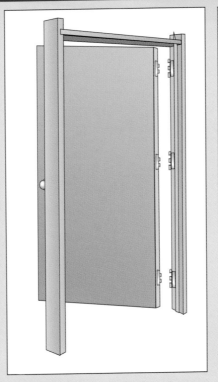

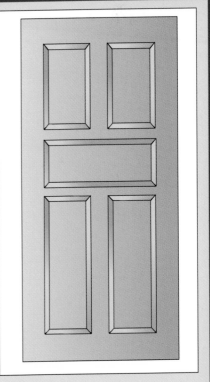

Prehung Doors Speed and ease of installation are the main reasons to use a prehung door: It comes wrapped with a jamb with hinges installed and pre-bored holes for a lockset.

Standard Doors Ability to customize and greater choices justify the effort it takes to install a standard door. A jamb must be built, hinges installed, and holes drilled for the lockset.

Panes and Screens

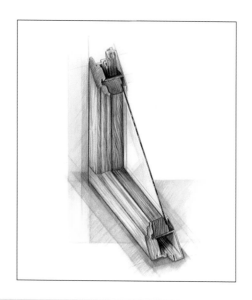

Single-pane The least energy-efficient window is the single-pane variety (*see drawing at right*). Common in older homes, this type of window is suitable only in mild climates. A better choice is double- or triple-pane windows; *see below.* One option that can help with a single-pane window is to have a low-E coating applied to the pane. This coating filters out UV rays to protect furnishings while also helping to insulate the home in winter and summer.

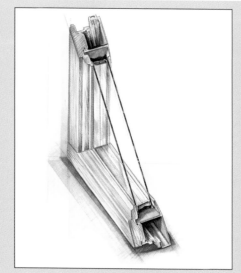

Double-pane A double-pane window, like the one *shown here,* has two panes of glass separated by an air space. When sealed properly, this air space provides insulation from both summer heat and winter cold. To further increase the insulating properties of the window, some manufacturers inject a safe, colorless gas (such as argon) into this space. A quality gas-filled double-pane window with low-E coatings typically provides an R-value (insulation rating) of around 4 to 5.

Illustrations on pages 26–27 courtesy of Weathershield, © 2001

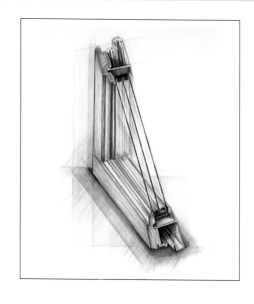

Triple-pane The ultimate in insulated windows is the triple pane (*see the drawing at right*). Three panes of glass offer two separate insulating spaces. Here again, these spaces can be filled with argon or other gas to increase the insulting properties. R-values around 10 are common with triple-pane windows. A side benefit of both double- and triple-pane windows is that they also significantly reduce noise transmission. The drawback to both of these is that they're more expensive than single-pane windows.

GRILLE OPTIONS

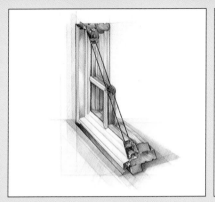

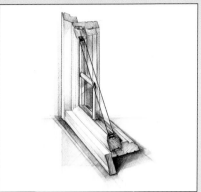

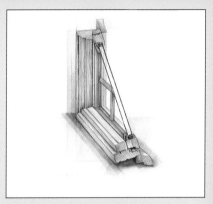

Simulated Simulated divided windows are sort of a hybrid of the air-space and perimeter grilles *shown at right.* As in the air-space, spacers fit inside the panes; and as with the perimeter, grilles are affixed to the exterior, but here they're permanently attached.

Air-Space On windows with air-space grilles, the grilles are inserted during manufacture in the air space between the panes. A choice of bar widths and profiles is available, and since they're sealed between the panes, cleaning is a snap.

Perimeter Perimeter grilles attach to the exterior of the glazing. They snap into place by way of a concealed pin system to quickly upgrade the appearance of a plain window; they also readily snap out for easy cleaning.

SCREENING OPTIONS

Two different options for screening materials are available to choose from: fiberglass and aluminum. Each has its plusses and minuses. On the plus side, fiberglass screening is very easy to install and is inexpensive. Some fiberglass screening manufacturers produce screening that also serves as a sun screen or shade. On the minus side, fiberglass screening damages easily and tends over time to work loose from the rubber splines that hold it in place on the screen.

Aluminum screening is more difficult to work with—it's stiffer and not as easy to cut, costs a bit more, and does not offer protection from the sun. On the up side, it's very tough, stays put (because it's often

stapled in place), and lasts a long time. With this in mind, I always recommend aluminum screening for screens (particularly screen doors) in homes where pets and children are present.

Fasteners

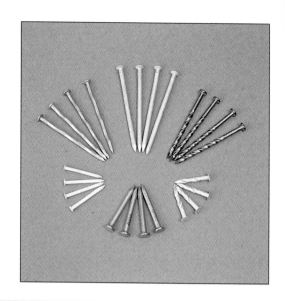

Nails Since the nails used for exterior window and door installations are exposed constantly to the elements, they should be made from corrosion-resistant metals (like aluminum) or else galvanized to prevent rust. Shown here (*clockwise from top left*): 8d hot-dipped galvanized threaded nails, for a better grip than straight-shank nails; 10d aluminum sinker nails; 8d stainless steel threaded nails; 1" oval-head aluminum trailer nails; 9-gauge hot-dipped galvanized joist hangers; and 1¼" aluminum trim nails (available in white or brown to match your trim).

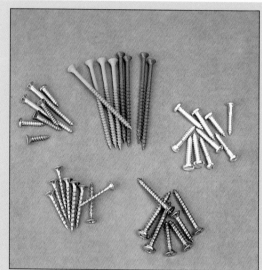

Screws Screws for window and door installations are also best made from corrosion-resistant metals or galvanized. Shown here (*clockwise from top left*): brass wood screws in a variety of sizes; coated deck screws, which come in two colors (light green to blend in with pressure-treated lumber, and light tan for natural woods); solid aluminum straight-shank screws; stainless steel panhead screws; and hot-dipped galvanized straight-shank screws. I recommend stainless steel or hot-dipped galvanized screws because they're tough and won't strip out like aluminum and brass screws tend to.

VINYL-COATED SCREWS

A newcomer to the fastener market, vinyl-coated screws are touted as weather-resistant. The screws are coated with a thin layer of vinyl that seals the metal against the elements. This works great as long as the coating is not disturbed. The problem with these is that when you drive the screw through a piece of wood, it rubs off the coating; *see the photo at right*. This isn't a problem if the shank of the screw is encased in the wood. But it can be bad news if there's a gap between the pieces. Air will begin corroding the unprotected area. If this is a possibility with an installation you're working on, stick with hot-dipped galvanized screws—they'll hold up better over the long run.

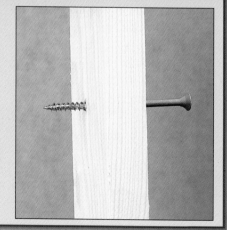

Locksets

Interior Locksets for interiors are easily identified since they aren't keyed (*see the photo at left*). Instead they feature two solid knobs, or one solid knob and one with a twist- or push-button-style lock. Nonlocking sets are used for hallway doors or any door that doesn't require controlled access. Twist-style or push-button-style locksets are used for rooms where privacy is desired. If you purchase a locking type, make sure there's a small hole in the center of the nonlocking knob: This allows you to release the lock from the outside in case you get locked out.

Exterior If you're looking to purchase an exterior lockset, buy quality. Pay a bit extra to get a solid, high-quality lockset. This is one piece of hardware that you don't want to skimp on. Not only is the security of your home an issue, the exterior locksets in a house most often receive the hardest use. Pay a little more to get one that will last a lifetime. A quality set like the one *shown here* can range from $50 to $100. For added security, consider buying a package that combines a lockset and a deadbolt that are keyed the same.

DECORATIVE OPTIONS

The variety of decorative locksets available nearly matches the wide variety of doors the homeowner has to choose from. Your front door can have a huge impact on the overall impression your house projects. A quality lockset that blends in well and complements the décor will make the door fit in with the intended look. A poor choice in a lockset can create a disjointed or haphazard look. If you can't decide among a number of locksets, buy them all and bring them home. Have a helper hold each one up to the door, stand back, and see how it looks. Once you've decided on the best set, return the others.

Weatherstripping

Self-adhesive foam Of all the window and door weatherstripping products, self-adhesive foam is the quickest and easiest to apply. Simply peel off the protective backing and press the foam in place. Self-adhesive foam comes in a variety of widths and thicknesses. It can readily be cut to length with a pair of scissors and will turn a corner easily. Look for closed-cell foam when buying this type of weatherstripping, as it won't absorb moisture. Be aware that self-adhesive foam is not the hardiest of weatherstripping; it needs to be inspected every season and replaced if worn out.

Gaskets Rubber gaskets, like the ones *shown here,* are both flexible and long-lasting. They cost more than self-adhesive foam and require more effort to install, but they'll last a lot longer. Gaskets are available in coils in white and brown and are attached to a window or door frame with small nails or brads. A common application for this style gasket is between a door and a door stop. Make sure to keep tension on the gasket as you install it to prevent bumps, which can cause a loss of seal.

Expanding foam Although technically not weatherstripping, expanding foam is often useful in door and window installations to fill large gaps. Expanding foam comes in pressurized canisters with a spray tube to dispense the foam. You'll find two rates of expansion to choose from: standard and minimal expansion. Since it's often difficult to judge how much standard-expanding foam will expand, many homeowners prefer minimal-expanding foam. Whichever you use, wear gloves (this stuff is really sticky) and fill the cavity in short bursts, allowing the foam to expand fully each time.

Caulk

Caulk is used on a regular basis for window and door installations, for repair work, and for routine maintenance (such as fall weatherstripping inspections) to seal gaps between the units themselves and their surrounding frames. Caulk is also used extensively in new window and door installations to fill gaps between rough openings and jambs, to fill in between stops and replacement windows, and to fill spaces between metal frames and window casings on replacement storm windows.

Types Caulk comes in tubes to fit a caulk gun so it can be applied quickly and with some accuracy. It's also available in smaller squeeze-type tubes for touchup work. Acrylic latex is used to fill gaps behind trim prior to painting; silicone is often used in exterior applications, such as when caulking around a window or door, because it stays flexible over time. Pure silicone is the most flexible, but it won't take paint. A hybrid—siliconized latex—offers better flexibility than plain latex yet can be painted. *See the chart below* for common caulks and their applications.

Types of caulk

Material	Application
Acrylic latex	Most common application is filling gaps and voids behind trim; also known as painter's caulk, as it accepts paint well; inexpensive and very easy to use and clean up
Butyl rubber	Where you need to seal metal (such as flashing to masonry); inexpensive, flexible, but very messy to use (wear disposable rubber gloves)
Silicone	Wood-to-masonry applications; bathroom tile joints that won't be painted; extremely flexible and long-lasting, but can't be painted
Siliconized acrylic latex	Interior and exterior applications that require a more flexible caulk; bonds better to surfaces and lasts longer than acrylic latex; less messy and easier to use than silicone

Chapter 3
Framing Windows and Doors

The first step to installing a new window or door, whether it's in an existing wall or a new one, is to build a rough opening to accept the unit. The key word here is *rough;* openings for windows and doors need to be slightly oversized for a few reasons. First, even if you're extra careful when installing the framing members, odds are that they won't all be perfectly level and plumb. Making the opening oversized still allows you to insert the unit and then shim it so it's level and plumb prior to fastening it to the frame. Second, clearance between the unit and framing makes it easier to slip in a demolition blade in case you want to remove the unit in the future. Third, all wood moves in response to changes in humidity—the extra clearance allows the framing and unit to swell and contract without binding.

For the most part, framing openings in interior walls (usually for doors) is a fairly straightforward process. Exterior walls, on the other hand, provide a challenge—after all, you will be knocking a hole in the side of your house. Granted, this can be rather nerve-wracking, even for an experienced DIY'er. But as long as you carefully follow a set sequence and take your time, it's readily doable by the average homeowner.

In this chapter, I'll start by thoroughly describing the rough opening requirements for both windows and doors (*opposite page*). Then I'll take you through the type of framing you'll likely encounter in your home: platform (*page 34*) or balloon (*page 35*). This is followed by an explanation of how a typical wall is constructed (*pages 36–37*) so that you'll be comfortable modifying one. Next, there's a section detailing when and why you should use temporary supports, and how to build and install them (*pages 38–39*).

Since you'll be removing existing studs to frame an opening for a door or window, you'll need to add a new framing system to assume the load previously handled by the studs. The heart of this new system is the header—the header spans the opening, and its size depends on the width of the opening; *see page 40 for more on this*. Once the opening is complete, jambs are installed to provide a finished surface (*page 41*).

In the last section of this chapter (*pages 42–47*) I'll take you through the process of installing a rough opening in an exterior wall one step at a time—everything from removing the existing wall covering and adding temporary supports to framing the opening and removing the exterior siding.

Rough Openings for Doors and Windows

Whenever you need to add a window or door to a wall, you'll need to frame a rough opening. Stud placement is critical here for the window or door to fit properly. In most cases, the rough opening should be ½" to ¾" wider and taller than the unit you're installing (consult the manufacturer's instruction sheet for the recommended gap). This extra space allows you to adjust the unit for level and plumb with shims. In no case should you frame the opening for a wider gap. If you do, the fasteners you use to secure the unit may penetrate only into the shims and not into the jack or trimmer stud.

Doors The blue arrows *in the drawing at left* identify the finished opening of the door. The green arrows show the rough opening. The framing members you'll need to install are: the king studs first, the jack or trimmer studs, and the header. Note that there's a gap at the bottom of the door for the threshold that may be installed later, or may come as part of the unit if it's a prehung door.

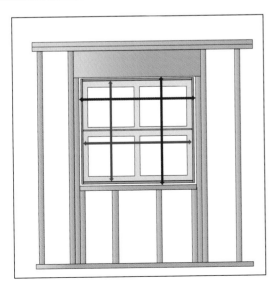

Windows Just as in the drawing for the door, *above,* the blue arrows indicate the finished opening and the green arrows define the rough opening. The framing members for a window are similar to that for a door: king studs, jack studs, and header. The only difference is the addition of cripple studs beneath the sill plate and above the header (if the header doesn't completely fill the space above the window). King studs are installed first, followed by jack studs and then the header. The opening is completed by adding the cripple studs.

Platform Framing

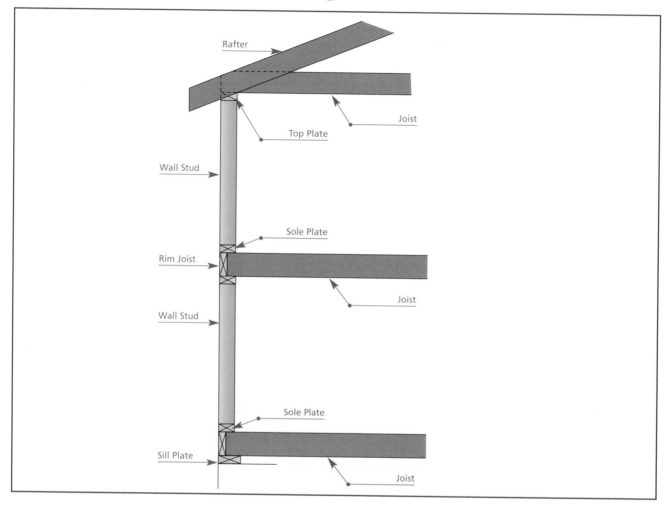

Platform framing is the most common construction method used today to build homes and other structures. A platform-framed structure is built one story at a time; each story is built upon a platform that consists of joists and a subfloor; *see the drawing above.* When one story is completed, the next platform is built, and construction on the second story can begin.

The separate platform of each story, technically the sole plate and top plate of each layer, eliminates the primary disadvantage of balloon framing—the lack of fire stops (*see page 35 for more*

on this). The top and sole plates also provide convenient nailing surfaces for the installation of drywall and other wall coverings. Platform framing uses less wood than other methods, maximizes interior space, eliminates bridging, and allows single-layer floors and simpler corner posts—it's no wonder this method is the most popular.

Balloon Framing

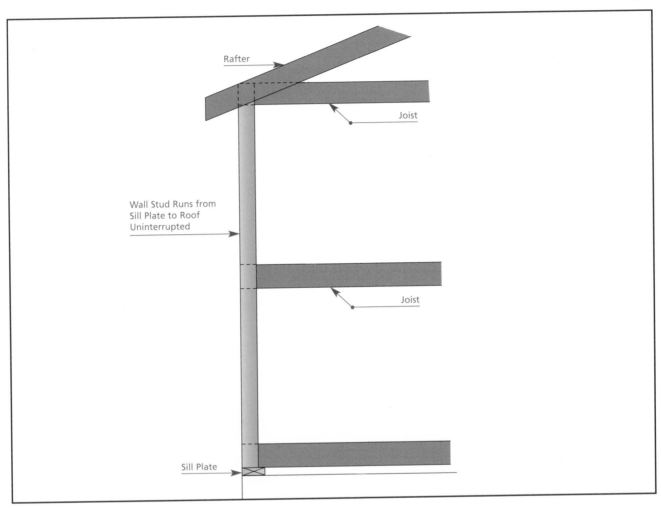

Rafter

Joist

Wall Stud Runs from
Sill Plate to Roof
Uninterrupted

Joist

Sill Plate

The identifying feature of a balloon-frame structure is that the wall studs run unbroken from sill to roof, no matter how many stories the structure has; *see the drawing above.* This creates a membrane-like or balloon-like frame. Although many older homes were constructed this way, balloon framing for houses has been superseded by the newer platform framing method (*see page 34*).

In its day, balloon framing offered a number of advantages over the post-and-beam structure: It took advantage of man-made nails, which were a lot cheaper than hand-pegged joinery; it used inexpensive standardized lumber; and it created stable exteriors that were easily covered with stucco and other materials.

But balloon framing had some problems. First, blocking (fire stops) needed to be added in the vertical wall cavities to prevent fires from spreading from floor to floor. Also, insulating this type of wall was difficult because it usually opened into the basement at the sill.

Basic Wall Construction

Basic wall construction is fairly simple: Typically studs are spaced 16" on-center and tied to a single sole plate attached to the subfloor and one or two top plates. In the past, these framing members were often 2×4 stock. This helped standardize many of the wall framing practices. But today, with our greater emphasis on energy efficiency, more and more homes are being built with 2×6 framing. This has a couple of advantages. First, the deeper wall cavity allows for thicker, more energy-efficient insulation to be installed. Second, since the studs are beefier, they can be spaced at 24" intervals instead of every 16".

Exterior walls are heavily insulated and have a vapor barrier installed on the warm side of the wall (typically a thin sheet of continuous plastic) to prevent moisture from entering the house. The cold side of the wall can be further insulated with rigid foam board, over which the siding is then installed. Interior walls are often left uninsulated and are covered directly with drywall or another wall covering.

The standard height for ceilings is 8 feet. Since the ceiling covering cuts into this height, you can't install a full 4×8 sheet of drywall to the walls without trimming it. The accepted solution to this is to frame the walls slightly higher (typically 8 feet, ¾"). If you were to subtract the thickness of a double top plate and a single sole plate, you'd end up with 7 feet, 8¼" (92¼") for the length of the wall studs. Most lumberyards offer studs precut to this dimension to make framing walls even easier.

Common wall terms

Term	Definition
Blocking	Horizontal blocks inserted between studs every 10 vertical feet to prevent the spread of fire in a home
Cripple studs	Short vertical studs installed between a header and a top plate or between the bottom of a rough sill and the sole plate
Double top plate	A double layer of 2-by material running horizontally on top of and nailed to the wall studs
Header	A horizontal framing member that runs above rough openings to take on the load that would have been carried by the wall studs; may be solid wood, be built up from 2-by material, or be an engineered beam such as MicroLam or GlueLam
Jack stud	A stud that runs between the sole plate and the bottom of the header; also referred to as a trimmer stud
King stud	The wall stud to which the jack stud is attached to create a rough opening for a window or door
Rough sill	A horizontal framing member that defines the bottom of a window's rough opening
Sheathing	Panel material, typically plywood, that's applied to the exterior of a wall prior to the installation of siding
Sole plate	A horizontal 2-by framing member that is attached directly to the masonry foundation or flooring; also referred to as a sill plate or mudsill
Stud	A vertical 2-by framing member that extends from the bottom plate to the top plate in a stud wall
Top plate	A horizontal 2-by framing member that's nailed to the tops of the wall studs

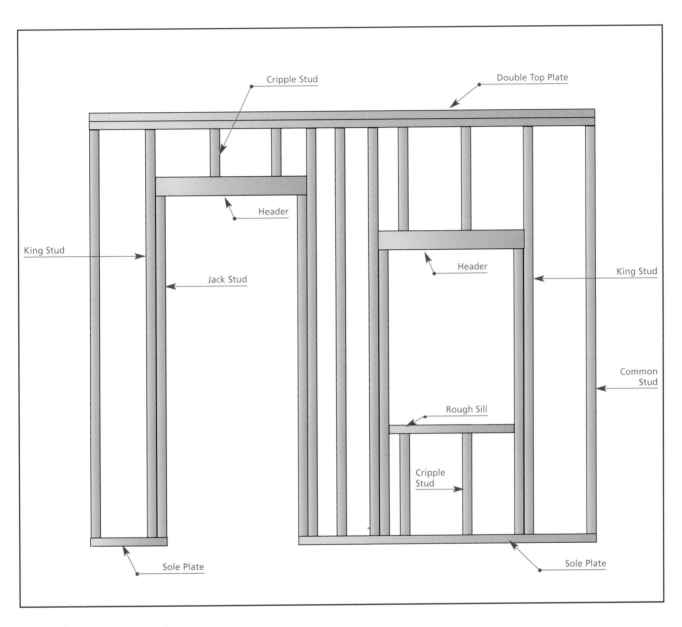

Cripple Stud

Double Top Plate

Header

King Stud

Jack Stud

Header

King Stud

Common Stud

Rough Sill

Cripple Stud

Sole Plate

Sole Plate

Anatomy of a Wall

A typical 2-by wall consists of vertical wall studs that run between the sole plate attached to the subfloor and the top plate or double top plate; *see the drawing above.* Whenever an opening is made in the wall for a window or door, a horizontal framing member called a header is installed to assume the load of the wall studs that were removed. The header is supported by jack studs (also referred to as trimmer studs) that are attached to full-length wall studs, known as king studs. The shorter studs that run between the header and the double top plate or from the underside of the rough sill of a window to the sole plate are called cripple studs.

Temporary Supports

Whenever a remodeling job requires that you remove a load-bearing wall or remove more than one stud in a load-bearing wall, you'll need to make temporary supports. The temporary supports bear the weight that the wall normally would, until a new support system can be installed (such as a new header or beam). The type of temporary support you use will depend on your house framing (platform or balloon) and whether the joists run perpendicular or parallel to the wall you're working on. With platform framing, the easiest way to support the wall is to build a T-shaped support structure that can be used for either parallel or perpendicular joists (*see below*). The structure is pressed into place with hydraulic jacks (*see page 39*). Note: If you're planning on removing a load-bearing wall, you'll need to add support on each side of the wall. Balloon framing is supported by adding a temporary support header (often referred to as a whaler); *see the sidebar on page 39 for more on this.*

Platform The temporary support platform is placed under the ceiling joists roughly 3 feet from the wall to be removed or supported. As you can see in the photo *at right,* the support mimics a standard wall by providing a sole plate, a top plate, and support beams (in this case, 4×4s).

Anatomy To make a temporary support platform, start by measuring the rough opening you're planning on (or the width of the wall to be removed) and add 3 to 4 feet to this so the support will extend out past the opening. Cut three 2×4s to this length (or one 2×4 and a 4×4, *as shown here*). The 4×4 will be a double top plate and the single 2×4 is the sole plate. To protect the ceiling, add a layer of carpet or carpet padding to the top of the top plate. For best results, glue this in place instead of using nails or staples, since these can scratch a painted surface.

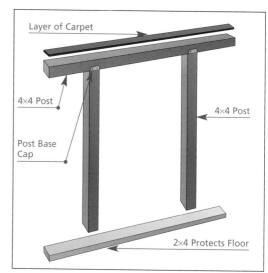

Layer of Carpet

4×4 Post

4×4 Post

Post Base Cap

2×4 Protects Floor

Build To build the temporary support, place a pair of hydraulic supports on the sole plate and measure from the top of the jack to the ceiling. Subtract 4" for the top plate, and cut the posts to length (these can be one 4×4 or a pair of 2×4s nailed together). Attach the posts to the top plate about 2 feet in from each end. I use metal post base caps to join the parts. Use plenty of 2"-long screws or nails to secure the base caps to the posts and top plate.

Jacks For perpendicular joists, start by slipping a tarp under the temporary sole plate to protect the floor. Then place the jacks on the sole plate and, with the aid of a helper, lift the support onto the jacks. Adjust the posts so they're plumb, and raise the jacks up until the top plate just barely begins to raise the ceiling. Be careful: Too much pressure here and you'll damage the ceiling. For joists that are parallel to the wall, bolt a pair of 4×4 cross braces to the top plate 1 foot in from the ends and cut posts that are 8" less than the jack-to-ceiling distance. Position the sole plate directly over a floor joist, and lift and raise the support as you would for perpendicular joists.

SUPPORTING BALLOON FRAMING

Balloon framing requires a different type of support mechanism. Instead of a T-shaped brace and hydraulic jacks, a temporary header (called a whaler) is bolted to the wall studs and supported by temporary jack studs. To support a balloon-framed wall for a new opening (such as a door or window), start by removing the wall covering from floor to ceiling. Then cut a whaler (a 2×8) about 4 feet longer than the rough opening you've planned. Then temporarily attach it to the studs so it's flush with the ceiling. Cut a pair of jack studs to fit snugly between the floor and the whaler, and attach them to the whaler with nailing plates. Next, drill holes in the whaler and bolt the whaler to the wall studs, using 3½" lag screws. Finally, drive shims under the jack studs to support the whaler firmly.

Headers

Headers are used to span the tops of doors and windows and are sometimes referred to as lintels. They are designed to bear the weight that would normally be distributed by the wall studs that were removed (to make room for the window or door). The header is supported by jack studs, often called trimmer studs or vertical trimmers. These run alongside and are fastened to a king stud. Cripple studs connect the header (and rough sill if a window is being installed) to the top plate (and sill plate for windows). Headers can be cut from 4×4 stock for a 2×4 wall, or they can be built up using a variety of methods. Some local codes also allow headers to be cut from MicroLam and GlueLam (engineered beams). The width and length of the header will be determined by your local building code, so it's important to check your code before planning any framing work that involves windows or doors. (*See the chart below for typical sizing.*)

Placement Headers for windows are most often placed the same distance down from the ceiling as the header for a door (*see the drawing at right*). Although this isn't required by code, it usually looks the best and it simplifies both layout and construction. The other advantage to placing headers like this is that it makes it easier in the future to convert a window into a door, since the existing header may be able to be used as the door's header.

Header spans

Size	Grade (Douglas fir)	Maximum Span (in feet)
4×4	#2	4
4×6	#2	6
4×8	#2	8
4×10	#2	10
4×12	#2	12
4×14	#1	16

Jambs

A jamb for a window or door is installed inside a rough opening to create a finished surface. In addition to this, stops are added to window jambs to allow the window sash to move up and down independent of each other and to control where the door stops when it's closed. Stops also provide a convenient place to install weatherstripping to ensure a weathertight seal between the door, stop, and jamb. Jambs for windows are complicated, and so for the most part they come preinstalled with the window unit. Doorjambs, on the other hand, are simpler and are available separately, or come preattached in the case of a prehung door (*see page 25 for more on this*). Most home centers stock precut doorjamb kits for 36"-wide doors. You'll need to trim them only if the rough opening isn't standard height or if the door is less than 36" wide. If necessary, measure and cut the jamb pieces to length following the manufacturer's directions. Then attach the top jamb to the side jambs with finish nails.

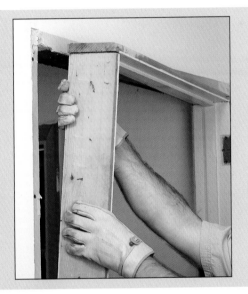

Shimming and leveling Insert the assembled jamb in the rough opening so it will end up flush with the wall covering you'll be installing—typically you'll offset it ½" from the framing members to allow for ½" drywall. Add carpenter's shims as needed to plumb and level the jamb. Use the shims in pairs, and insert them from opposite sides of the jamb. Check the jamb constantly as you adjust the position of the shims. For doors, make sure to shim behind the hinges and near the lockset for maximum support.

Securing the jamb When the jamb is level and plumb, secure it to the framing members by driving screws or finish nails through the jamb and shims and into the jack studs or trimmer studs. Make sure to use nails or screws that are long enough to penetrate the jamb and shims and into the framing—typically a 2½" to 3" length will do. Score the shims with a utility knife and snap off the excess.

Framing a Rough Opening

1 **Remove inside wall covering** The first step to framing a rough opening for a window or a door is to locate the framing members and remove the interior wall covering to expose them. An electronic stud finder will make quick work of locating the studs. Before you begin on the wall, pry off baseboards or moldings as necessary. When removing drywall, cut through the tape at all corners and down the length of the wall at the studs with a utility knife to minimize tearing. Once the wall covering is removed, pull out the insulation between the studs and remove any exposed nails.

2 **Add temporary supports** In any situation where you're planning on removing more than one wall stud in any exterior wall or in an interior load-bearing wall to make way for a new rough opening, you'll need to build and install temporary supports. Temporary supports prop up the wall in the short term while the existing studs are removed and new studs and a header are installed. *See pages 38 and 39* for detailed instructions on how to do make and use temporary supports.

3 Cut framing members Once the temporary supports are in place, you can cut the framing members that you've marked for removal. There are a number of ways to do this. A reciprocating saw will quickly zip through the studs and fits easily between them. A circular saw set at maximum depth also works well, as does a handsaw or "toolbox" saw powered with a little elbow grease. Note: If you're planning on reusing any of the studs, make your cut near either the top plate or the sole plate. If not, cut them in the middle, as this gives you the best "handle" to remove each piece.

4 Cut partial cripple studs Here's a timesaving trick I learned from a renovator friend of mine—instead of removing the wall studs completely, cut them near the top to create cripple studs. To do this, simply measure down the correct height down from the ceiling and cut the wall studs to create cripple studs. They're already spaced the correct distance apart and affixed securely to the top plate. All you'll have to do is toenail the bottom of each to the header once it's installed.

EXPOSED STUD TIP

If you're removing only a section of a wall, here's a simple tip that will save you some work. Instead of cutting the sole plate and top plate flush with the stud that will remain, leave a bit exposed for the stud or studs that you'll be attaching to the existing stud.

For non-load-bearing walls, leave 1½" of sole or top plate exposed (*as shown here*). For load-bearing walls, leave 3" exposed for the double 2×4 or 4×4 post that will be installed.

5 **Remove parts** After you've cut all the wall studs, they can be removed. Wearing leather gloves, grip each piece, bend it back toward you, and twist it. In most cases, this will release the stud from the nails holding it in place. If not, lever it back and forth while twisting at the same time. Stubborn studs may need a pry bar or crowbar to convince them to give up their grip. Be careful of exposed nails in the top and sole plates. Bend over any exposed nails to reduce the chances of injury.

6 **Locate new king stud** Whenever possible, you should use one of the existing wall studs as one of the two king studs that define the rough opening. To locate the second king stud, you'll need to do a little math. Say, for instance, you're installing a 36"-wide door. Add 1" to this for the two ½"-thick jambs, and ½" for clearance—this means that your jack studs need to be 37½" apart. Now add 3" to this (for the two jack studs), and your second king stud needs to be 40½" away from the first. Measure over, cut a king stud to length, and toe-nail it to the top and sole plates.

7 **Install jack studs** Next, cut two jack studs to length; typically these will be 80" (standard door height) less the thickness of the sole plate (1½") or 78½". Face-nail one of these to each of the king studs. It's a good idea now to remeasure the width of the opening and the actual width of the door to make sure it will fit in the rough opening. Measure the distance from the bottom of the sole plate to the top of the jack stud, and compare it to the actual height of the door and jamb to make sure it will fit as well.

8 **Install header** Once the jack and king studs are in place, you can build and install the header that will fit on top of the jack studs. Measure the span between the king studs, and consult the header chart on *page 40* to determine the width (height) of the header. Measure and cut the header components to length (typically two pieces of 2-by material with a layer of ½" plywood sandwiched in the middle), and screw or nail them together. Then position the header and toenail it to the king studs.

9 **Add cripple studs** If you removed all the existing wall studs in Step 5, you'll need to install cripple studs between the header and the top plate. Measure the distance between the two, and cut short cripple studs to length. Face-nail one to each king stud and then space the remaining cripple studs 16" on-center and toenail them to the header and top plate. Alternatively, if you cut the old studs to length to leave cripple studs (*Step 4*), all you need do is toenail them to the header. Note: Now it's safe to remove the temporary supports you installed in Step 2.

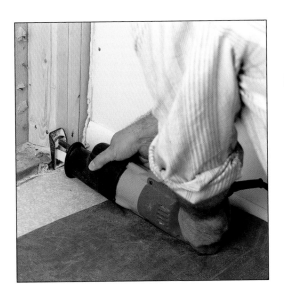

10 **Cut the sole plate** Once you've removed the temporary supports, the next step is to cut the sole plate so that it can be removed. A reciprocating saw works great here—especially if you invert the blade *as shown.* This way it'll cut almost flush with the subfloor. A short "toolbox" saw also does a fair job here, but because the exterior wall prevents a full stroke, it takes many shorter strokes to fully cut through the sole plate. Whichever tool you use, concentrate on keeping each cut perpendicular to the king studs.

11 **Remove sole plate** To remove the sole plate, insert the end of crowbar under one end and pry it up. In most cases, you won't get a clean break because it's almost impossible to saw completely through the sole plate. Don't worry about this now; just get the bulk of the sole plate out of the way. Then you can go back with a chisel and a mallet and trim away any remaining fragments. Here again, it's important to keep these chisel cuts perpendicular to the king studs. **Safety Note:** Remove any exposed nails in the subfloor immediately to prevent a puncture.

12 **Nail at corners** At this point, you should have a properly sized rough opening in the interior wall. All that's left is to remove the external siding or wall covering. Although this sounds simple enough, it's a bit complicated and can be nerve-wracking. The secret to success here is taking your time and double-checking each of the steps before moving on to the next. The first step is to define the opening. To do this, start by driving a 16d nail through the wall covering at each corner of the opening.

13 **Chalk line around perimiter** Now you can move to the exterior of the house. Locate the tips of the four nails you drove through the wall covering, and beginning at one nail, wrap the chalk line around the outside edges of each nail. This will define the perimeter of the opening. To transfer this outline onto the exterior covering of the house, simply snap each of the lines in turn a couple of times. Remove the chalk line, measure the width and length of the opening, and compare these measurements to the actual rough opening.

14 **Attach 1×4 to siding** The next step is to cut through the exterior wall covering. The most common exterior is siding (*shown here*). Since siding doesn't offer a flat surface for a circular saw to ride on, it's best to attach a 1×4 temporarily to the exterior to create a flat reference. Cut the 1×4 so it's about 12" longer than the height of the opening, to provide support at both ends of the cut. Either position the 1×4 an inch or so away from the chalk line and make a freehand cut, or place it on the line and use its edge as a guide.

15 **Cut through siding** My tool of choice for cutting through a wood exterior is a circular saw fitted with a carbide-tipped demolition blade. It'll cut right through nails as it cuts the siding. Set the saw blade so it will just cut through the thickest part of the siding. To start the cut, angle the saw so the front of the saw base is on the 1×4 and the back end is raised up. Retract the blade guard, turn on the saw, and lower the blade into the siding to make a plunge cut. Then guide the saw along the chalk line, making sure to stop when you reach a marked corner.

16 **Remove siding** After you've made the first complete cut, move the 1×4 to the opposite side and repeat for the other side. Do this for the top and bottom cuts as well. Since you stopped near the corners, you'll need to complete these cuts with a handsaw or reciprocating saw. Have a helper handy to support the wall covering as you make these cuts and remove the siding. If necessary, use a sharp chisel and a mallet to square up each of the corners. Now you're ready to install the door or window—*see Chapters 4 and 5* for detailed instructions on how to do this.

Chapter 4
Windows

As I mentioned in Chapter 1, windows can have a huge impact on the overall impression a house gives. This is both good and bad. It's good if the windows are in good repair, were chosen to complement the décor, and work properly. On the other hand, if the windows are tired and worn-out looking, in a state of disrepair, and/or don't work, it's bad. Fortunately, replacing a window isn't a big chore, as long as the new window is a direct replacement, or you're using one of the new-style replacement windows that require virtually no modifications to the existing walls or framing.

In this chapter, I'll show you how easy it is to replace a window, starting with how to remove the existing trim (*opposite page*). Then, if you're installing a same-sized new window, I'll take you through the steps required to remove the old one (*page 50*). Note that if the window you're planning to install is not the same size as the existing window, you'll need to alter the rough opening before installing the new window. The instructions for building a rough opening for a door (*see pages 42–47*) can be adapted to frame an opening for a window. The only difference is that you'll need to install a sill and support it with cripple studs (*see page 33 for more on this*).

Next, I'll show you how to install a replacement window, one step at a time (*pages 51–55*)—everything from removing the old sash to shimming and securing the new window. I think you'll be pleasantly surprised to see how easy this really is. Glass block windows, while not suitable for every room, do fit in extremely well in bathrooms and entryways; on *pages 56–57,* I'll cover how to install one of these.

An easy way to increase the insulation values of your windows is to install a combination storm (*pages 58–59*). These nifty units store two storms and a screen within the frame, so there's no more trudging up and down the stairs twice a year for seasonal switching. Shutters, while they won't affect how well your windows work, can enhance how they look. *See pages 60–61* for step-by-step directions on how to install decorative shutters. Window trim, on the other hand, can help with both looks and insulating properties by blocking drafts caused by gaps between the window jamb and wall covering. I'll go over the different types and show you how to install them (*pages 62–63*). Finally, there's a section on how to weatherstrip your windows to cut down on heating and cooling losses (*pages 64–65*).

Removing Trim

Whenever you're faced with removing or replacing a window, your first task will be to remove the existing trim pieces. Removing trim requires care and patience. Even if you're not planning on reusing any of the pieces, you'll want to take precautions to prevent damage to the wall as the trim is pried off; *see below.* This is particularly essential when dealing with walls covered with drywall, because they're prone to denting. It is easy to get carried away removing trim—to just grab a section and rip it off the wall—but before you do this, take the time to slice through any paint between the trim and the wall with a utility knife. In many cases, especially in older homes where the walls and trim have multiple layers of paint, paint can form a strong bond between the trim and the wall. If you don't cut this paint "joint," it's quite likely that you'll tear off the paper covering of the drywall as you remove the trim. The last thing you need in a home improvement job is to create additional work for yourself.

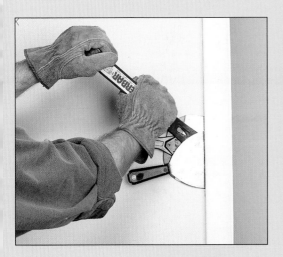

Use pry bar If you're planning on salvaging the trim, it's best to remove it with two putty knifes and a pry bar, *as shown.* Slip one putty knife against the wall, and insert a stiff-blade putty knife between it and the trim. Now insert a pry bar between the two and gently pry the trim away from the wall. This takes a bit longer, but it will prevent damage to both the trim and the wall. For situations where you know you won't be reusing the existing trim, you can remove it quickly with a pry bar. With cove base molding, loosen a corner with a putty knife and pull.

Pull out nails If you're planning on reusing any of the wood trim from the wall or wall section, don't pound the nails out through the face of the molding. All this usually accomplishes is splitting the wood, which creates a larger hole to fill once the trim is in place. Instead, pull the nails out from behind with a pair of locking pliers, *as shown in the photo at left.* This will create only a small hole to fill. Make sure to wear leather gloves to protect your hands from sharp nails and splinters.

Removing a Window

1 **Cut through nails** After you've removed the trim, you can remove the unit. One of the quickest and most effective ways to release a window from the framing members is to cut through any nails or screws with a reciprocating saw fitted with a demolition blade, *as shown in the photo at right.* A couple of things here: First, you've got to have clearance for the blade—too tight an opening will result in kickback and bent blades. Second, make sure to press the saw firmly against the wall as you cut and keep a firm grip when you encounter a nail.

2 **Pry off brick molding** The next step (if the window is an exterior unit) is to remove the exterior brick molding from the framing members. Here again, a pry bar will make quick work of this. Make sure to wear leather gloves while removing the brick molding to protect your hands from nails and splinters (*see photo at right*). If you're planning on reusing the brick molding, protect it from damage from the pry bar by slipping a stiff putty knife behind the molding, as described for removing trim on *page 49.*

3 **Pull unit out** At this point the window should be free and ready to be removed. If it isn't, stop and find out what's holding it in place. Quite often there's a hidden nail or screw you missed. For larger windows, have a helper on hand as you pull it out of the rough opening. A pry bar may be needed to persuade a stubborn unit to come out smoothly. Note: If you're removing an older double-hung window with sash weights, remove the sash weights by first cutting through the sash cord and then pulling out the weights.

Installing Replacement Windows

If you've ever wanted to replace old, worn-out windows but were afraid of the work and the cost involved, consider replacement windows. I really like these units because you can replace an old window with a low-maintenance replacement window in one afternoon. The beauty of replacement windows is that you don't have to disturb the interior or exterior wall coverings. All you do is remove the old sash—you leave the existing jambs in place—and then insert the new window. Although there are more steps to it than that, it really is a simple process. And with the cost of a standard replacement window in the $100 to $150 range, it's well within the budget of the most homeowners. Although you might think the installation part is the critical portion of the job, it's actually measuring and ordering the correct-sized window. Fortunately, this isn't a complicated task; *see the sidebar below.*

1 Remove old storm window The first step in replacing a window is to start by removing any existing storm windows or combination storms (*as shown here*). Combination storms are typically held in place with aluminum screws around the perimeter of the window, or they may be held in place with aluminum transition strips. In either case, remove the screws (and transition strips if necessary) and lift out the window. Combination storms that have been in place for years may require a little persuasion to come out; a tap or two on the frame with a rubber mallet from the inside will usually do the job.

MEASURING FOR REPLACEMENT WINDOWS

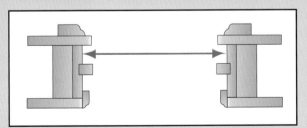

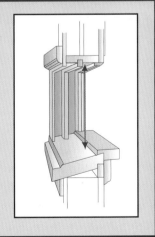

Width Measure the width of the opening behind the trim or stops from one side jamb to the other. Take this measurement in three places: at the top, middle, and bottom. Use the smallest of these dimensions.

Height Measure the height from the bottom of the sill to the head jamb above the trim. Here again, take this measurement in three places: at each side and in the middle. Use the smallest of these dimensions.

2 Remove inside moldings With the exterior storm window removed, you can turn your attention to the interior. Start by removing the inside moldings. Since you'll most likely be reusing these, you'll need to take them out carefully. Begin by severing any paint bond between the stops and the jambs by slicing through it with a utility knife. Then slip a stiff putty knife between the stop and the jamb and pry it from the jamb, beginning at the bottom and working toward the top.

3 Remove lower sash Once you've removed the interior moldings, the lower sash will be free for removal. To remove the sash, you'll need to first disconnect its counterbalance system, then lift it out of the window. The counterbalance will be a sash cord, a spiral balance, or the spring from a block-and-tackle balance. **Safety Note:** Take care as you release any of these balances because they all will be "in tension." I've found locking-jaw pliers to be the most reliable way to grab the spring or sash cord so that you can carefully disconnect it from the jamb and feed it back into its housing.

4 Pry out parting stops With the lower sash out of the way, the upper sash can now be removed. To free it from the window jamb, you'll need to remove the parting stops from the side and head jambs. As this stop is typically set into the jamb, it requires a bit more leverage to remove. Since you won't be reusing these, you don't have to worry about damaging them. The quickest way I've found to remove them is to drive a chisel into the stop and then use this to lever the stop out far enough so that I can slip a putty knife in to pry it out completely.

5 **Remove upper sash** Now that the parting stops have been removed, the upper sash can be taken out. Here again, you'll need to first remove its counterbalance. After you've lifted out the upper sash and set it aside, remove any remaining parts of the counterbalance. For spiral balances, unscrew and take out the tube that houses the balance and spring. Remove the mounting screws that secure block-and-tackle balances and the sash pulley, and lift them out. Tip: If the old window used sash weights, stuff some fiberglass insulation in the cavity where the weights were, to help prevent heat loss in the winter.

6 **Install starter strip** With both sashes and the counterbalance removed, the window opening can be prepared for the replacement window. Start by removing any hook eyes or other protruding fasteners, and then thoroughly clean the side jambs, head jamb, and sill. At this point, you can install a starter strip if one was supplied in your window kit. The starter strip is typically an L-shaped strip that acts as a stop when you're installing the new window. Install it on the outer sill about ⅛" from the blind stop. Caulk the inside edge of the stool and the outside along the sill angle.

7 **Caulk inside edges of blind stop** To get a tight seal between the top, bottom, and sides of the replacement window and the old jamb, apply a ⅜" bead of silicone caulk along the inside edges of the blind stops. Apply the caulk to the top stop and on both sides. Note: Here's where the cleaning you did in Step 6 will pay off— silicone caulk will not adhere well to the stops if they're not clean.

8 **Install header expander** Even though many residential windows are standard sizes, many are not. To compensate for variance in size, some replacement window manufacturers provide a header expander. The expander slips over the top of the replacement window and can be raised or lowered to fill any gap between the top of the window and the head jamb. The header expander is nothing more than a U-shaped piece that snaps into place on the top of the window (*see the photo at right*).

9 **Tilt in new window** Ah...the moment of truth. If you measured correctly and the window is the right size, the new window should slide easily into the opening. You should have about ½" combined clearance between the sides of the new window and the jamb. This space allows you to slip in shims and level the window (*Steps 10 and 11*). Note: If there's a gap at the top of the window, slide the header expander up until the gap is filled. Wait to install screws to secure it until after you've leveled the window.

10 **Check for level** In order for the sash in the new window to operate properly without binding, it's important that the window be installed level and plumb. Check for this with a long level on the sides and a shorter torpedo level on the top and bottom. Most likely, the window will need some adjustment to bring it into alignment; *see Step 11.*

11 **Insert shims and secure window with screws** To adjust the new window for level and plumb, insert shims in the gap between the sides of the new window and the jamb. Install the shims wherever the manufacturer has predrilled holes for mounting. Slide the shims back and forth and in and out until the window is level and plumb. Then secure the new window to the jamb with the mounting screws provided in the kit. Double-check the window with the level, and adjust the shim position as necessary. Cut off any protruding shims with a sharp utility knife.

12 **Replace the inside moldings** Now you can replace the interior molding you removed in Step 2. Remove any old nails in the molding by pulling them out through the back of the molding with a pair of locking-jaw pliers. Then position the molding and fasten it to the jamb using 2"-long finish or casing nails. Don't use the existing nail holes for this—the nail won't grip the wood sufficiently. Instead, drive the nails in a couple of inches from each hole. Then countersink the nails and fill these holes and the old ones with putty. When dry, touch up with paint.

13 **Caulk the outside** All that's left to complete the installation is to seal the exterior of the window. Apply a bead of paintable silicone caulk around the perimeter of the window, taking care to fill in any gaps between the existing jambs and the sides, top, and bottom of the new window. Smooth the caulk with a wet finger, and when it has dried, touch it up with matching paint.

A Glass Block Window

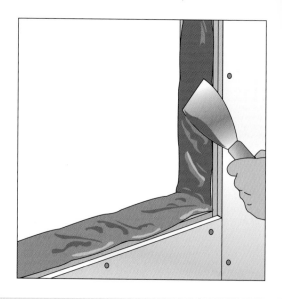

1 **Coat framing members** The first step in installing a glass block window is to protect the wood framing members with a thick coat of asphalt emulsion, *as shown in the drawing.* Note: It's also important to install an expansion strip (often made of cork or rubber) around the perimeter to leave room for the framing members to expand and contract due to changing levels of humidity. If you don't, the movement of the framing members could squeeze the block, causing it to break.

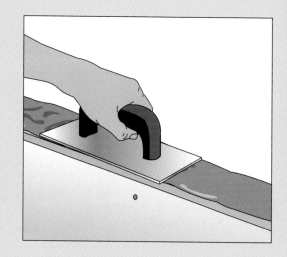

2 **Apply base mortar** After you've allowed the asphalt emulsion to dry the recommended time, the next step is to apply mortar to the base or sill of the window. Apply the mortar with a trowel or wide-blade putty knife and then level it with a mason's trowel, *as shown.* In most cases, you're looking for the layer to be about ½" in thickness. Take your time here to make sure the layer is uniform in thickness, since this serves as the foundation for all the blocks.

3 **Lay first row** Now you can begin installing the block. Set the first block in the corner, and tap it with the handle of your trowel or putty knife to embed it in the mortar. Then spread a layer of mortar onto the side of the block. Here again, it's important that the mortar be of uniform thickness. Set the next block in position and press it into the mortar. Continue in this manner until the first row is complete.

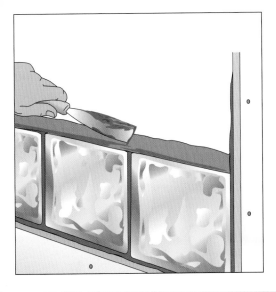

4 **Apply next mortar** Before you apply the next layer of mortar, check that the first row of glass block that you installed is level. Place a level horizontally on the row and check for level. If it's not level, tap the protruding block or blocks down with a rubber mallet. Check frequently with the level as you go. When it checks out, apply the next layer of mortar, making sure that it's of uniform thickness. Smooth it out with a mason's trowel to create a flat reference point.

5 **Additional rows** Install the next row of glass block as you did in Step 3. Continue adding layers of mortar and block until the window is complete. Remove any mortar squeeze-out with a trowel, and then go back and "tool" the joints by running a scrap of ¾" dowel along the joints. This will create a half-moon depression that will help the window shed water and also create a pleasing appearance. After the mortar has set up, apply a bead of silicone caulk around the exterior of window—this helps seal the window and still allows for expansion and contraction.

PREASSEMBLED BLOCK WINDOWS

To help speed up the installation of glass block windows, some manufacturers offer preassembled window units, *as shown at right.* These units are stocked at some home centers and can be special ordered from most. They come in a variety of sizes, and some offer built-in ventilation. Installation is straightforward: Just insert the unit in the opening, attach it to the framing members with the supplied hardware, and then apply caulk to seal any gaps.

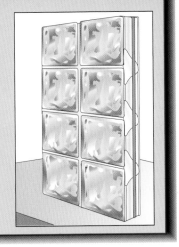

New Combination Storms

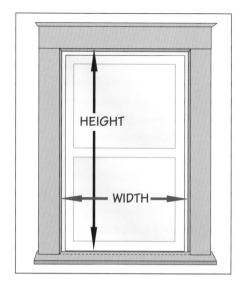

1 **Measure for new unit** Before you can install a new combination storm window, you'll need to measure and order a new unit. To measure the existing window, measure the width and height, *as shown,* to the nearest ⅛". For the height, measure from the inside edge of the top casing to the end of the side casing (where it rests on the sill). Take measurements in three places—at both ends and in the middle—and use the smallest dimension when ordering a new combination storm.

2 **Remove the old storm** If you're replacing an existing combination storm (*as shown here*) or an existing storm window or screen, remove the old unit. Older combination storms will either have a flange that's screwed directly to the jamb or casing, or be held in place with metal transition strips. In either case, remove the screws and then lift the unit out of the opening and set it aside.

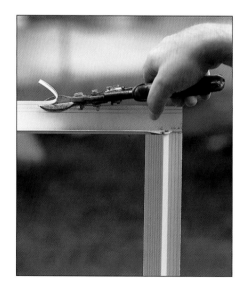

3 **Trim if necessary** I like to check the fit of the new combination storm at this point. Lift it into place and check to see whether it slides in easily. If too large, most combination storms can easily be trimmed to fit. The flanges on many aluminum combination storms are ribbed to make trimming with metal snips a simple task; *see the photo at right.* If you do need to trim a flange, start by trimming off the smallest amount. Then check the fit and trim more if necessary.

4 **Caulk the opening** Once you're sure the new storm fits well, you can apply caulk where the flanges make contact with the existing window frame. But before you do this, take the time to thoroughly clean the areas to be caulked. Scrape off any loose bits of paint and then wash the jamb with a mild soap solution. Allow the jamb to dry before applying the caulk. Use a high-quality silicone caulk and apply a ⅜" bead around the perimeter of the window *as shown.*

5 **Install the new unit** Now you can lift the new combination storm up into place in the opening. Once it's in position, work around the perimeter, pressing the flange into the opening so that it makes contact with the jamb and evenly distributes the caulk under the flange to create a waterproof seal. Use a clean, dry cloth to wipe up any caulk that squeezes out.

6 **Secure the storm** All that's left is to secure the storm to the existing window frame with the screws provided. In most cases the heads of these screws are painted to match the flange (such as the white ones *shown here*). Before you install the screws in the predrilled holes in the flanges, it's a good idea to check to make sure the storm window is level and plumb. I usually secure the top of the frame to the jamb with a single screw in the center hole, then place a torpedo level on the bottom frame, pivot the frame until it's level, and install the remaining screws.

Installing Decorative Shutters

There are two basic types of shutters you can mount on windows: working shutters and decorative shutters. Since glass isn't as precious as it once was, most homeowners don't feel the need to "shutter up" the home every time a storm is brewing. Although most homeowners don't need the protection that working shutters afford, most still like the look of shutters. With this in mind, shutter manufacturers have moved away from working shutters and now primarily make decorative shutters that mount permanently to a home's exterior. Since modern shutters don't need to protect windows, they're most often made of low-maintenance plastic. They're available in a wide variety of styles, colors, and sizes and are stocked at most home centers.

1 **Position the shutter** The first step to installing a set of shutters is to unpack the shutter and position it next to the window. Have a helper stand behind you to help find the best position in terms of both the distance away from the window and how the shutter is positioned top to bottom. Once you've located the ideal position, make a set of marks on the exterior wall so that you can relocate the shutter easily.

2 **Drill mounting holes in shutter** Most shutters do not have predrilled mounting holes. That's because they don't know what type of exterior covering your home has. For flat surfaces such as stucco or brick, hole placement is simple: Just drill pairs of mounting holes near the top, bottom, and middle. If your home has siding, you'll need to be more careful: You'll want to locate the holes at the high point of the siding so that the shutter is fully supported when installed. Follow the manufacturer's instructions as to recommended hole placement and diameter.

3 **Drill holes in exterior** Now you can use the shutter as a template for drilling the holes in the exterior. Simply align the shutter with the marks you made in Step 1 and drill through the shutter into the wall. For wood siding, use a twist bit or brad-point bit. If you're drilling into masonry, use a carbide-tipped masonry bit. If you've got a lot of shutters to install in masonry, consider renting a hammer drill, a special drill that combines rotary action with percussion to drill holes quickly in tough materials.

4 **Insert mounting hardware** Once you've drilled all the holes in the exterior for the shutter, carefully insert the mounting hardware—typically a special plastic bolt that's ribbed to grip the interior of the hole. Slip the bolt through the shutter and gently press it into the hole in the exterior wall. Make sure to press in straight and don't allow it to bend in the process—these have a tendency to snap quite easily. Continue pressing the bolt in until it's flush with the surface of the shutter.

5 **Tap in place** All that's left is to tap the bolt in place with a hammer to firmly secure the shutter to the exterior wall. Be careful here: In many cases, a single tap of the hammer will do. Remember that the shutter is plastic and will bow and crack if you drive the bolt in too far. Once you've got one shutter in place, repeat the process for the other side, taking care to have someone help you align one shutter with the other.

Window Trim

Installing window trim, or "trimming out" a window, can be done numerous ways. The two most common methods, square-cut and miter-cut, are shown *below*. The available varieties of trim, or casing as it's often called, are almost as numerous as styles of windows to choose from—everything from plain, simple molding to high-profile fancy trim. What you choose is really a matter of taste. A lot will depend on whether or not you want to match the other trim in the room.

When buying trim, be aware that there are a number of grades available. Paint-grade trim is made by gluing up short pieces of wood that are joined to make long pieces. Since the joints can be obvious, this trim should be painted. (Note: Some home centers and lumberyards sell pre-primed trim—all you need to do is brush on a topcoat.) Stain-grade trim offers less variations in grain and color and so is designed to accept a stain nicely. Since it costs more than paint-grade, make sure you buy it only if you're intending to stain the trim; otherwise, buy paint-grade.

Square-cut A common form of window trim in older homes is the square-cut, *as shown here*. This style of trim consists of a top, two side pieces, a stool, and an apron. The main advantage to this system is that since all the cuts are square and the pieces are butted together, it's easy to install. The disadvantage to this is that it leaves wood grain exposed on the trim pieces on the sides of the window. The stool is installed first, followed by the apron and the trim (or casing).

Miter-cut The most common style for attaching trim in modern homes is the miter style, *shown here*. It's often referred to as picture frame trim because it resembles the frame of a picture. Miter-cut trim is more of a challenge to install because the 45-degree miter cuts must be accurate for the frame parts to come together with no gaps. The advantage to this style of trim is that no end grain is exposed—the wood grain appears to run continuously around the perimeter of the window.

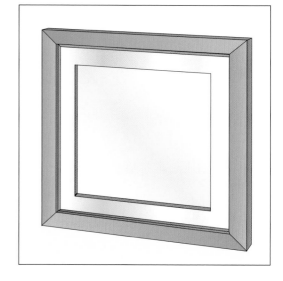

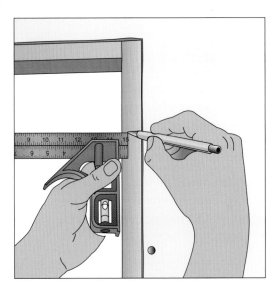

1 **Mark reveal** To install miter trim, start by marking the reveal on each jamb. A reveal is a slight offset between the trim and the jamb. It allows for easier installation and also provides a shadow line for visual interest. The easiest way to mark this is to set the blade of a combination square so that it protrudes ⅛". Then place a pencil against the blade of the square, press the head of the square against the jamb, and run these around the perimeter to mark the reveal.

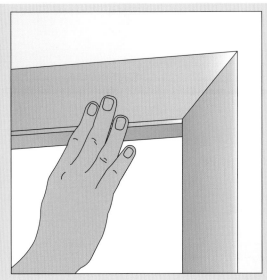

2 **Install vertical trim first** I like to measure, cut, and install the trim starting with the vertical pieces. Place a piece of trim in position so its inside edge is flush with the marked reveal. Then make marks at the top and bottom of the trim where the horizontal and vertical reveal lines meet. Once these are cut and installed (*Step 3*), move on to the top and bottom trim pieces. Measure these by running a tape measure between the installed side pieces, and cut pieces to fit. Note: If your window isn't square, start long and sneak up on the cut, adjusting the saw angle as necessary.

3 **Install the trim** My tool of choice for installing trim is an air-powered nailer like the one *shown in the drawing at left.* An air nailer drives and sets the nail in the blink of an eye. Not only does this eliminate the extra step of having to countersink the nails with a nail set, it also prevents the trim piece from shifting out of position—a common problem when attaching trim with a hammer and nails. If you don't own one of these and you've got a lot of trim to install, consider renting one.

Weatherstripping

If the windows in your home are of the older, single-pane, double-hung variety, odds are that you're losing a lot of heat in the winter and coolness in the summer through small gaps around the window. If you can't afford more-efficient replacement windows (*see pages 51–55*), you can at least seal the gaps with weatherstipping. Air typically enters around the windows through gaps behind the trim, between the sash and the jambs, around the stops, past poor glazing, and even through the pulleys of double-hung windows. There are numerous weatherstripping products available for windows, and it's important to match the type to its job. V-strips are best used to seal moving parts like the sliding sash in a jamb. Foam works best for parts that close against each other, like the bottom of a sash and the windowsill.

Foam on sash bottom One of the simplest but often overlooked ways to help weatherproof a window is to add a compressible foam strip to the bottom of the sash. Most foam strips are self-adhesive. They'll form a good bond with the sash as long as it's clean and dry. Take the time to clean it thoroughly before you install the foam strips. Neoprene foam, although more costly, tends to last longer than standard gray foam.

Snaking plastic v-strips For the most part, plastic V-strips are easy to install: Just peel off the backing and press them in place. The tricky part to installing these is preventing the strip from prematurely sticking to the jamb. This is particularly a problem when slipping the strip up between the upper and lower sash. To get around this, cut the backing about a foot from the top. Then pull this up and over the top of the strip *as shown.* Now you can feed the end of the strip between the sashes. Lower the bottom sash, pull off the backing, and press it in place. Now you can raise the sash, remove the remaining backing, and secure the strip.

Installing v-strips: cut to length Metal V-strips are typically sold as coils of around 10 feet in length. They're a lot tougher then plastic strips and will hold up better over time. To install metal V-strips, start by measuring one of the sash stiles and add 2". Transfer this measurement to the V-strip and make a mark. Then, using a pair of metal snips, cut the strip at the mark.

Installing v-strips: attach with brads Unlike plastic self-adhesive V-strips (*see the opposite page*), metal V-strips are fastened to the window jamb with small brads. Start by raising the lower sash and position the strip in the channel. Make sure not to cover any sash-closing mechanisms. Fasten the V-strips to the jambs with the brads provided by the manufacturer. Since these are often very short, judicious use of needlenose pliers to hold the brads will save your fingers.

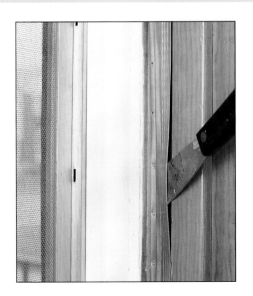

Installing v-strips: flare with putty knife To achieve the best seal, you may want to flare out the open ends of the V-channel slightly. Do this by inserting a putty knife into the strip and prying it gently open. Keep in mind that the greater the flare, the higher the risk will be of causing the window to stick as it opens and closes. Flaring the strip too far will also increase the chances of the sash catching on the strip and causing it to buckle.

Chapter 5

Doors

I have to admit, I enjoy working on doors more than I do windows. In the first place, they're a lot simpler mechanically. And second, since most interior and exterior doors come in only a couple of sizes, there's less confusion when ordering and installing them. Most doors are available in one of two heights: 6-6 or 6-8. This equates to 6' 6" (or 78") and 6' 8" (or 80"). Widths vary between 2-0 and 3-0; *see the chart below right.* Sliding and swinging patio doors are typically 80" tall and either 5' or 6' in width, 6' being by far the most common.

In this chapter I'll start by showing you how to remove a door (*pages 67–68*) in preparation for installing a new one. If you're planning on installing a door where there wasn't one previously, you'll need to frame a rough opening; *see pages 42–47* for detailed instructions on how to do this. Next, I'll take you through all the steps required to install a new exterior door—everything from installing the drip edge in order to help the door shed water, to adding shims in order to level and plumb the door (*pages 69–74*). This is followed by directions on how to install a prehung interior door (pages 75–77).

If the door you're installing is a hollow-core door (*see page 25*) and you need to trim it to fit,

I'll show you the steps involved in this process (*pages 78–79*). Installing a bi-fold door is covered on *pages 80–81,* and it's followed by one of the more challenging door installation projects— adding a sliding door. I'll take you through this somewhat complicated process one step at time on *pages 82–87.* The chapter concludes with instructions on how to install a storm door (*pages 88–91*), add door trim (*page 92*), install a new threshold (*page 93*), and add weather-stripping to your doors to help keep out the elements and reduce heating and cooling losses.

Common door sizes

Width Desigination	Actual Measurement
2-0	24"
2-4	28"
2-6	30"
2-8	32"
3-0	36"

Removing a Door

1 **Pry off trim** The first step in removing a door is to pry off the existing trim on both sides of the door. How you do this will depend on whether or not you want to reuse the trim. If you're not planning on reusing it, a pry bar like the one *shown here* will make quick work of the job. If, however, you want to salvage the trim, use a pair of wide-blade putty knives. Slip one knife under the trim, and then the other. The bottom knife will protect the wall covering while you gently pry off the trim with the other putty knife.

2 **Remove hinge pins** With the trim removed, you can turn your attention to the door itself. Start by removing the hinge pins. I generally start at the bottom hinge and work my way toward the top. Although most folks reach for a screwdriver and hammer to drive the pins out of the hinges, I recommend using a cold chisel instead. Some hinge pins can be extremely stubborn; the numerous hammer blows to a screwdriver will both mushroom the head and damage the tip. Reach for a cold chisel instead—it's designed for this kind of work.

3 **Remove door** After you've removed all of the hinge pins, you can detach the door. Swing the door open slightly to get a good grip, and lift the door up slightly and out—it should come away cleanly. If not, try pivoting either the top or bottom of the door away from the jamb to release it. Solid-core doors are surprisingly heavy, so consider having a helper on hand to help detach and move the door.

4 **Remove hinges** When most doors are installed, one screw on each hinge jamb is removed (usually the center one) and replaced with a longer screw that will pass through the jamb and into the jack stud in the rough opening to firmly support the door. Instead of trying to cut through these screws (*in Step 5*), it's easier to simply remove them. If in doubt as to which hinge screws are the long ones, just remove them all.

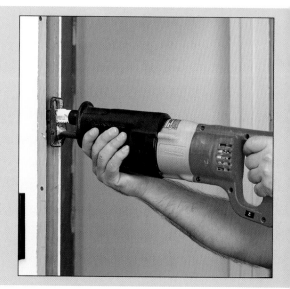

5 **Cut through the nails** To release the doorjamb from the frame opening, the next step is to cut through the nails that secure it to the framing members. The best tool for the job here is a reciprocating saw fitted with a demolition blade. Since these saws are powerful and can buck hard when they come in contact with a nail, it's important to press the cutting guide of the saw firmly against the wall as you make the cut. An alternative to cutting the nails is to pry them out. You'll need a cat's paw for this plus a lot of patience.

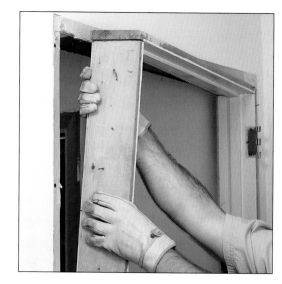

6 **Remove jamb** Once you've cut through the nails, the jamb should be free of the framing members. All that's left is to pull it out of the opening. Since you'll likely encounter nails that have been cut off, it's a good idea to protect your hands with leather gloves. Grip one of the side jambs firmly, and give it a tug to pull it out. After the jamb is removed, you can easily break it down for reuse or disposal.

A New Exterior Door

1 **Attach brick molding** If you are installing an exterior door where there wasn't one previously, you'll first need to frame the new rough opening and remove the exterior wall covering; *see pages 42–47 for instructions on this.* If you're replacing a door, first remove the old door; *see pages 67–68.* In either case, you'll most likely need to attach the brick molding to the doorjamb prior to installation if it didn't come preattached. Brick molding is available precut and pre-primed. All you need do is mark the reveal (*page 92*) and nail the molding to the jamb.

2 **Test the fit** With the brick molding in place, lift the door up and into the rough opening to make sure it fits well. Exterior doors tend to be rather heavy, so have a helper on hand to assist you as you lift and position the door. Once the door is in place, check to make sure you have sufficient clearance between both side jambs and the jack studs for the shims that you'll use later to plumb and level the door. As you lift the door in and out of the opening, be careful not to catch the jamb on the framing members, since it can easily splinter.

3 **Mark outline on siding** If the exterior wall covering on your home is siding, you'll need to remove some of it around the perimeter of the door in order for the brick molding to sit flush against the wall. To do this, start by tracing around the outside edge of the brick molding directly onto the siding with a carpenter's pencil or a marker. Go over these marks a couple of times to make them highly visible. Take care to keep the lines straight because the ridges of the siding tend to skew the pencil as you're marking.

4 **Cut away siding with circular saw** After you've marked the outline of the brick molding, carefully remove the door and set it aside. There are a couple of ways to cut the siding. I prefer to cut it freehand with a small trim saw (*shown here*). Another option is to first attach a flat reference board (as you did when cutting the opening; *see page 47*) and then guide a full-sized circular saw along the reference board to make the cut. For either method, try to split the marked line as you cut, and stop well before you reach each corner.

5 **Clean up the corners** As you complete the cuts on the two sides and above the header, the bulk of the cut-off siding will simply drop off. The siding near the corners, however, will need the attention of a handsaw first to complete the cuts, followed by a sharp chisel to clean up the corners. Be careful as you tap the chisel with a hammer or mallet—the siding may not be well supported and can crack or splinter. Take your time, and make light paring cuts with the chisel.

6 **Add roofing felt** Since exterior doors are exposed to the elements, it's important that you protect the internal framing members in case there's ever a breach in the weatherstripping or exterior caulking. The best way to do this is to apply a layer of roofing felt (felt paper) to the inside faces of the rough opening. Cut strips about 12" wide, carefully work the felt under the siding, and then wrap it around to cover the framing members. Staple the felt in place and trim it so that it's flush with the inside edges of the rough opening.

7 **Install drip cap** Another trick you can use to help foil Mother Nature is to install a drip cap at the top of the rough opening. A drip cap is a piece of extruded aluminum shaped in sort of an "L." It's designed to slip under the siding and will form a small lip to help funnel water away from the door. Simply cut the drip cap to length, apply a bead of silicone caulk to the edge, and force it up between the siding and the roofing felt you installed in Step 6. Once the door is installed, the drip cap will be locked into place.

8 **Caulk the threshold** The last thing to do before installing the door—and yet another way to keep out the elements—is to apply caulk to the threshold. Use a high-quality silicone caulk and apply it generously in a zigzag pattern, like the pattern *shown in the photo at left.* Remember: It's a whole lot easier to wipe off excess caulk than it is to remove the door after it's been installed and apply more caulk when you discover that the threshold leaks.

9 **Install the door** It's finally time to install the door. But before you do this, consider adding a little bit more insurance against the elements: Apply a bead of silicone caulk on the back side of the brick molding. This caulk will help fill any gaps between the brick molding and the roofing felt. Note: You'll also caulk around the brick molding once the door is completely installed (*Step 16 on page 74*). With the aid of a helper, lift the door up into position, taking care not to tear the roofing felt, and press it into place.

10 **Add shims** With the door in place, the next step is to add shims to level and plumb the door. Start by inserting shims behind each of the three hinges, behind the opening for the plunger for the door lockset, and at the top and bottom of the latch-side jamb. Also insert pairs of shims at the center and both ends of the head jamb. Insert the shims in pairs of opposing wedges, and adjust them in and out until they solidly fill the gap between the jamb and the framing members.

11 **Check for level and adjust** Hold a 4-foot level up against one of the side jambs and check it for plumb. Adjust the position of the shims until the jamb is plumb. Then move to the other side jamb and repeat the process. Finally, hold a small torpedo level up against the head jamb to make sure it's level. If any of these are off, the door won't open or close properly. Take your time here and double-check everything one more time before proceeding to the next step.

12 **Secure jamb to frame** Once you're satisfied that the door is level and plumb, you can secure it to the doorjamb. Your best bet here is a 2½"- to 3"-long casing nail. Make sure to drive the nail through the jamb only at the places where the shims are. The idea here is to drive the nail though the jamb and the shims into the framing members. This way the jamb will be fully supported. As you nail the jambs in place, check for plumb again with a level, and adjust the shims as necessary.

13 **Remove retaining bracket** Although you might feel that the door is firmly secured at this point, there are a couple more things to do before it's really rock-solid. The first thing to do is install long hinge screws (*Step 14*). In order for you to access the hinge screws, the door must be opened. All manufacturers of prehung doors install some sort of hardware to keep the door closed until it's installed. This may be as simple as a nail driven through the jamb and into the door, or a fancy retaining bracket (*like the one shown here*). In either case, remove it.

14 **Install long hinge screws** The prehung door you purchased should have come with three long hinge screws that are designed to lock the doorjamb firmly into the framing members. The door hinges may or may not have an empty slot waiting for these. If not, you'll need to remove one screw from each jamb hinge and replace it with a longer screw. If your door didn't come with these, go out and buy some 3"-long galvanized or coated deck screws and drive one into each hinge.

15 **Anchor brick molding** All that's left to secure the door is to attach the brick molding to the framing member. For this job, make sure that you use hot-dipped galvanized casing nails, typically 2½" to 3" in length. Drive nails through the face of the brick molding and into the framing member about every 12" or so. Then go back and countersink each nail with a nail set and fill the holes with an exterior-grade putty.

16 Caulk exterior There's one more job to do on the exterior of the door, and that's to apply a final bead of caulk around the perimeter of the brick molding. Use a high-quality paintable silicone caulk, and apply a generous bead where the brick molding meets the siding. Fill in any gaps as needed with the caulk, and then go back over the caulk with a wet fingertip to smooth it out.

17 Cut off shims and add trim To finish off the inside of the door, start by cutting off any protruding shims with a sharp utility knife (*see the photo at right*). Then you can trim out the door with the molding; *see page 92 for more on installing trim.* Finally, install the lockset of your choice (*see pages 100–102*) and test the operation of the door. If all went well, it should open and close smoothly, without binding, and create a solid seal against the elements.

ENCASED BLINDS FOR STEEL ENTRY DOORS

Here's a nifty product I found at the local home center—an encased mini-blind system for steel entry doors. These are a great way to add instant privacy to any door. Since they're encased, they don't slide around and bang into the door as it's opened or closed. But what I like best about these is that they mount directly to the existing window frame. You just remove the recommended screws from the existing window frame and replace them with longer screws to hold clips that secure the encased blind. You can raise and lower the blind and open and close the fins with the touch of a finger (*far right*).

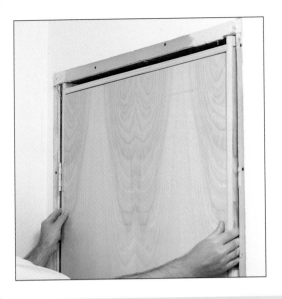

Installing a Prehung Interior Door

1 **Insert door in opening** Installing a prehung interior door is similar to installing an exterior door. The big difference is you're not constantly taking steps to seal and protect the door from the elements. If you're installing a new door where there wasn't one previously, you'll need to remove the wall covering and frame an opening; *see pages 42–47.* For a direct replacement, you'll need to first remove the old door; *see pages 67–68.* When the opening is prepared, check the fit of the new door.

2 **Shim** With the door in place, the next step is to add shims to level and plumb the door. Start by inserting shims behind each of the three hinges, behind the opening for the plunger for the door lockset, and at the top and bottom of the latch-side jamb. Also insert pairs of shims at the center and both ends of the head jamb. Insert the shims in pairs of opposing wedges, and adjust them in and out until they solidly fill the gap between the jamb and the framing members.

3 **Check for plumb** Hold a 4-foot level up against one of the side jambs and check it for plumb. Adjust the position of the shims until the jamb is plumb. Then move to the other side jamb and repeat the process. Finally, hold a small torpedo level up against the head jamb to make sure it's level. If any of these are off, the door won't open or close properly. Take your time here, and double-check everything one more time before proceeding to the next step.

4 **Secure jamb to frame** Once you're satisfied that the door is level and plumb, you can secure it to the doorjamb. Your best bet here is a 2½"- to 3"-long casing nail. Make sure to drive the nails through the jamb only at the places where the shims are. The idea here is to drive a nail though the jamb and the shims and into the framing members. This way the jamb will be fully supported. As you nail the jambs in place, check for plumb again with a level, and adjust the shims as necessary.

5 **Install long hinge screws** The prehung door you purchased should have come with three long hinge screws that are designed to lock the doorjamb firmly into the framing members. The door hinges may or may not have an empty slot waiting for these. If not, you'll need to remove one screw from each jamb hinge and replace it with a longer screw. If your door didn't come with these, go out and buy some 3"-long wood screws and drive one into each hinge.

6 **Cut off excess shims** After the door has been completely secured to the doorjamb and framing members, you can remove the excess shims. Cut off any protruding shims with a sharp utility knife (*see the photo at right*). For thicker shims, use a fine-tooth saw and be careful not to scratch the adjacent wall covering. Tip: One way to prevent damage to the wall coverings when sawing is to wrap a couple of turns of duct tape around the end of the saw. This keeps the sharp teeth from digging into the wall as you finish a stroke.

7 **Install trim** With the shims out of the way, you can turn your attention to the door trim. Start by marking the desired reveal on all the jambs. Then measure and cut the trim to length and install it with casing nails. *See page 92* for detailed instructions on how to install door trim. After you've countersunk and filled the nail holes (*Steps 8 and 9*), you can install the lockset of your choice (*see pages 100–102*) and test the operation of the door. If all went well, it should open and close smoothly, without binding.

8 **Countersink nails** There are only a couple of steps left to put the finishing touches on your new door. First, you'll need to countersink the trim nails with a nail set (*see the photo at left*). In most cases, each nail will only need a tap or two of the hammer. What you're looking for here is to set the head of the nail about ⅛" below the surface. This provides plenty of space for the putty to bond well to; any deeper, and you run the risk of splitting the trim.

9 **Apply putty** After all the nails have been set, go back and fill each hole with an interior putty. There are two basic types of this: one version that sets up and hardens, and another that doesn't. The type that hardens is best applied a bit proud of the surface so that you can sand it flush once it sets up. This type can be painted or stained as desired. The nonhardening variety should be applied only after the finish coat is wiped on, since it's usually chosen to match the existing finish and can't be painted or stained. Apply this type of putty so that it's flush with the surface.

Trimming a Hollow-Core Door

1 **Score the outer skin** A hollow-core door consists of two veneer "skins" attached to a wood frame with strips of cardboard inside, on edge, to support the skins. This presents a problem when you need to trim the door. If you need to remove less than 1", just trim it off. If you need to take off more, you'll need to remove the bottom frame piece and reglue it into the door after it's been trimmed. To help prevent the skin from splintering as it's cut, mark the cut line and then score it with a utility knife.

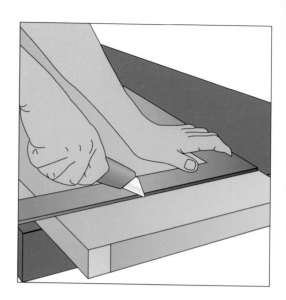

2 **Attach straightedge** Although you can try to cut the door freehand, I recommend using some type of a straightedge to guide the saw as it cuts. The straightedge *shown here* is a commercially available unit that has built-in clamps that grip the edges of the door. You could clamp a straight piece of scrap wood to the door instead. Make sure to take into account the offset required by the base of the circular saw as you position the straightedge.

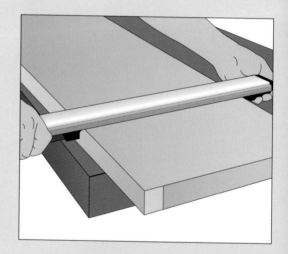

3 **Trim off excess** With the straightedge in place, you can trim the door to length. A circular saw fitted with a carbide-tipped blade works best for this. As you cut the door, make sure to press the base of the saw firmly against the straightedge to guide the saw. Keep the saw moving at a steady pace to prevent the saw blade from burning. Support the cutoff with your free hand as you finish the cut to keep it from splintering off.

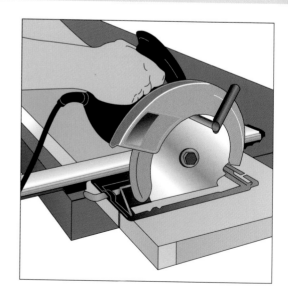

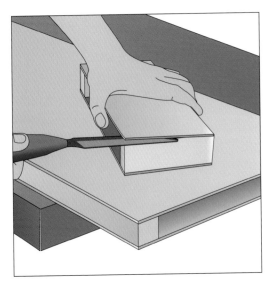

4 **Remove skin from cutoff** Now that the door is trimmed to length, the next step is to remove the frame piece from the bottom of the cutoff so that you can install it in the cavity in the bottom of the trimmed door. Use a wide, sharp chisel to carefully pry the skin off each face of the frame piece. Don't worry about damaging the skins, but take care not to gouge the frame piece. When both skins are off, use the chisel to remove any excess glue or wood fragments from the frame piece.

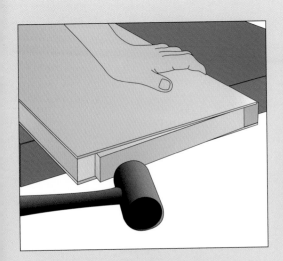

5 **Insert frame piece in door** Before you can insert the frame piece in the cavity in the door, you'll need to clear away any cardboard strips inside the door near the bottom to make room for the frame piece. Check the fit of the cleaned-off frame piece to make sure it slides easily into the bottom of the trimmed door. If it's a good fit, apply a coat of yellow carpenter's glue to both faces of the frame piece and slip it into the cavity in the door. You'll most likely need to persuade it with a few taps of a mallet to get it to seat fully.

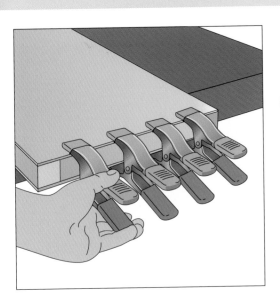

6 **Apply clamps** All that's left is applying clamps to the skins to press them firmly against the frame piece to ensure a good bond. Spring clamps (*as shown here*) work great for this. C-clamps also work well, but you'll need to protect the door skins from damage by slipping scraps of wood under the clamp pads before tightening them. After the glue has dried overnight, remove the clamps and scrape off any glue squeeze-out with a sharp chisel.

Installing a
Bi-Fold Door

1 **Install track** Instead of using hinges, a bi-fold door opens and closes via a set of pins in the top and bottom of the door sections. One set of pins allows the unit to pivot; the remaining set rides inside a track to guide the door sections. Installing the U-shaped track is the first step to installing a bi-fold door. Position the track centered on the doorjamb and up against the side jamb where it will pivot. Use the track as a template to mark mounting holes. Then drill pilot holes and screw the track to the jamb.

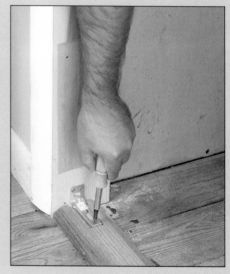

2 **Attach bottom bracket** Inside the track you'll find an adjustable bracket with a hole in it for one of the pivot pins (we'll adjust its position in Step 5). The other pivot pin fits into an L-shaped bracket that's attached to the floor and side jamb. The only critical thing to installing this is to make sure that like the track, it's centered on the jamb. Drill pilot holes and use the screws provided to fasten it to the flooring (or threshold) and side jamb.

3 **Add pins to door** With the pivot brackets in place, you can install the pins in the door sections. Each of the pins may be different: The top pivot pin is usually spring-loaded, the lower pivot pin is serrated to grip the ridges in the bottom bracket, and the track pin is often smooth, high-impact plastic. Follow the manufacturer's directions to install the pins in the door sections so that the door will swing open the way you want it to. Tap each of the pins in gently with a hammer—don't drive them in too forcefully, or you'll crack the door casing.

4 **Install door** Once the pins are in place, the door can be installed. To do this, start by fully opening the door. Then guide the top pivot pin into the hole in the track bracket and make sure the track pin is in the track. Next, pivot the bottom of the door into the opening while lifting up the door. This will depress the spring-loaded top pin, allowing you to lift the door up far enough to set the bottom pivot pin into the hole in the bottom bracket. Test to make sure the door pivots smoothly and closes fully. If it doesn't, it's easy to adjust; *see Step 5.*

5 **Adjust if necessary** There are three adjustments you can make to a bi-fold door to fine-tune how it operates. If the edge of the door section near the side jamb rubs up against the jamb, loosen the adjusting screw in the top bracket and move the door away from the side jamb. Once this is working properly, the bottom of the door needs to be aligned with the top pivot point. In most cases, all you have to do to adjust its position is lift the door up and move the serrated pin to align it. Finally, you can raise or lower the entire door by adjusting the bottom pivot pin up or down.

HIDING A METAL TRACK

Although the metal track that comes with a bi-fold door is functional, it's not very attractive. Here's an easy way to conceal the track and make it blend in with your décor. All it takes is a piece of ³/4"-round molding cut to match the length of the track. Attach the molding to the head jamb with finish nails, countersink and putty the nail holes, and paint it to match the trim (*see the photo at right*). If your trim is natural wood (like red oak), you can find ³/4"-round molding in a variety of natural woods in stock at many home centers and lumberyards.

A New Sliding Door

Installing or replacing a sliding door is one of the more challenging door projects. That's because the panels are big and heavy, there are a lot of moving parts, and adjusting the sliding panel can be tricky. On the plus side, a newly installed sliding door can totally change the look and feel of a room. Not only will a sliding door provide access to a deck or porch, it also lets in tons more light while affording great views. As long as you follow the manufacturer's directions carefully, the installation should go smoothly. The critical thing, of course, is that your rough opening must be sized correctly and also be square (*see pages 42–47*). It's also important to note that on most sliding doors, only one panel slides. Be aware that these panels are usually reversible—that is, you can make either the right- or left-hand panel be the active or sliding panel. All that's required to do this is to remove the wheel mechanism in one end of the panel and replace it in the opposite end (read the manufacturer's directions on how to do this).

1 **Assemble frame** Depending on the type of sliding door you purchased, it may or may not come in separate components. The unit that's being installed *here* came in three packages: a fixed panel, a sliding panel, and the frame and hardware. The first step is to assemble the frame. Following the manufacturer's directions, attach the side jambs to the head jamb and then to the sill, taking care to use the appropriate screws. If you're replacing a sliding window, you'll need to remove the old unit; *see pages 49–50.*

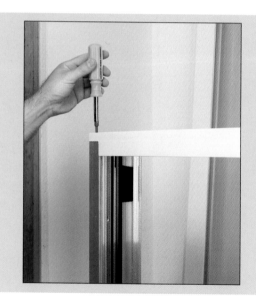

2 **Install flashing** Since exterior doors are exposed to the elements, it's important that you protect the internal framing members in case there's ever a breach in the weatherstripping or exterior caulking. The best way to do this is to apply a layer of roofing felt to the inside faces of the rough opening. Cut strips about 12" wide, carefully work the felt under the siding, and then wrap it around to cover the framing members. Staple the felt in place and trim it so it's flush with the inside edges of the rough opening.

3 **Caulk threshold** Yet another way to protect the door, the flooring, and framing members from the elements is to apply caulk to the threshold. Use a high-quality silicone caulk and apply it generously in a zigzag pattern, like the one *shown in the photo at left.* Remember: It's a whole lot easier to wipe off excess caulk than it is to remove the door after it's been installed and apply more caulk when you discover that the threshold leaks. You should also caulk in the corners of the frame where the jambs meet the sill.

4 **Install frame** With the opening prepared, you can insert the frame. Although the frame is fairly stable at this point, it can be damaged if it's accidentally racked. To prevent this, have a helper assist you in carefully positioning the frame in the opening. Once you've got it near the opening, tilt the frame and set the sill against the flooring. Then pivot the frame up so that it slips into the opening. Check to make sure that you've got sufficient clearance between both side jambs and the jack studs for carpenter's shims.

5 **Shim and secure** Insert pairs of shims wherever the frame is predrilled for installation screws and behind the lock keeper to prevent the frame from buckling. Hold a 4-foot level up against each jamb, and adjust the shims until the jamb is plumb. Then drive the screws provided in the kit through the predrilled holes, through the shims, and into the jack studs. Double-check each jamb as you secure it to make sure it's still plumb. An out-of-square frame will not allow the sliding door to operate without binding.

6 **Secure the threshold** After you've secured the side and head jambs, you can fasten the threshold to the sill. Depending on what the flooring or subflooring is made of, you may need to drill pilot holes for these screws. If in doubt, go ahead and drill these. It takes only a few minutes and will help avoid stripped screws. Make sure to use the shorter screws that are supplied in the kit for this purpose. When it's secured, apply a bead of caulk in the outside corners where the side jambs meet the head jamb.

7 **Install fixed panel** Now that the frame is secured, you're ready to install the panels. The fixed panel goes in first. The easiest way to insert either of the panels is from the outside. Note: Since these panels have double-insulated panes, they're quite heavy—have a helper on hand to assist you as you insert them into the frame. Insert the top of the panel into the outside slot in the frame. Then lift up the panel far enough so that the bottom of the panel clears the ledge of the sill. Once it clears, set the bottom into the outside sill slot. Do not slide the panel all the way over to the side jamb at this time.

8 **Install latch set in active panel** Before you install the active panel, most manufacturers suggest that you install the latch set and door handles to make it easier to slide the panel back and forth in the later stages of the installation. In most cases, the handle and latch hardware have their own directions. Follow these to install the latch (if not preinstalled by the manufacturer) and both the inside and outside handles.

9 **Install frame keeper** The latch set fits into a metal bracket often referred to as a frame keeper. The frame keeper is attached to the side jamb with a pair of screws that penetrate the jamb and go deep into the jack stud. Follow the manufacturer's directions for placement and installation. After the wheels of the fixed panel are adjusted (*see Step 11*), it may be necessary to adjust the position of the keeper up or down for the latch to engage properly. This isn't a problem, since the keeper is typically slotted to allow for easy adjustments.

10 **Install sliding panel** Once the latch and handles are in place on the active panel, you can install it in the frame. Before you do this, however, make sure that the wheels in the active panel are pushed up into the panel—this provides more clearance. Insert the top of the panel in the frame slot, then lift the panel up to clear the ledge in the sill. Set the panel down carefully so that both sets of wheels rest on the runner in the sill track.

11 **Adjust wheels** If you notice that the active panel is slightly askew, or that it doesn't slide smoothly, either of the two wheel assemblies may need adjustment. Following the manufacturer's directions, use a screwdriver to turn an adjustment screw on each assembly. Typically, you'll turn the screw clockwise to raise the panel and counterclockwise to lower it. Make these adjustments in small increments, and check the operation of the panel between adjustments.

12 **Slide fixed panel over** Now that both panels are in the frame, you can position the fixed panel and lock it into place. To do this, start by sliding the active panel into the jamb as far as it will go. Engage the lockset so that it firmly grips the frame keeper to hold the door in place. Then slide the fixed panel in the opposite direction to create a complete interlock of the panels (*see the photo at right*).

13 **Secure fixed panel to jamb** At this time you can secure the fixed panel to the jamb. This is typically done with a pair of clips located on the interior of the frame. These clips are fastened first to the fixed panel and then to the jamb. Position the top clip just under the head jamb and the bottom clip just above the sill. Depending on the manufacturer, you may or may not need to drill pilot holes for these clips.

14 **Install threshold sill cover** To prevent damage to the sill, most sliding door manufacturers provide a sill cover that creates a solid, flat surface to step on. The threshold sill cover is inserted between the side jamb and the fixed panel by inserting it into the fixed panel's track. You may find it necessary to trim this a bit to achieve a good fit; you can use a hacksaw, a pair of metal snips, or a metal file for this. The sill cover *shown here* is designed to snap in place—no screws or fasteners needed.

15 **Install the screen** Many sliding doors come with screens; on others they're an accessory that can be purchased separately. To install a screen door, place the top of the door in the channel in the head jamb. Push the door up to compress the top rollers, then, while holding pressure on the top rollers, swing the bottom of the door into the bottom track. Compress each of the two bottom rollers, and place the groove of the roller over the bottom track. If necessary, adjust the wheels with a screwdriver to raise the door off the track.

16 **Install strike plate** When you've adjusted the wheels in the screen so that the door is parallel to the side jamb of the door frame, you can install the strike plate that locks the screen door in place. Locate the strike plate on the side jamb, following the manufacturer's directions, and fasten it to the jamb with the screws provided. Slide the screen door closed and check the operation. Since most strike plates like these are slotted, they're easy to adjust up or down to engage properly.

17 **Caulk the exterior** The final step in installing your new sliding door is to seal any gaps in the exterior in order to keep out the elements. Apply a generous bead of paintable silicone caulk around the perimeter of the frame, taking care to fill in gaps between the door frame and the exterior wall covering. When you're done, smooth the caulk with a moistened fingertip, and once it has set up, touch up the area with house paint that matches your exterior.

A New Storm Door

1 **Prepare door** Most metal storm doors are shipped with the frame temporarily attached to the door via a set of shipping clips. You can remove plastic shipping clips by pushing in on the clips and then sliding them out of the frame. Metal clips (*like the one shown here*) are held in place with screws. The clip is screwed both to the frame and to the door itself. Check the manufacturer's directions before discarding the screws—they may be needed later on.

2 **Remove glass inserts** Depending on the type of storm door you've purchased, you may or may not want to remove the glass panes or "inserts" from the frame. Most manufacturers suggest removing the glass insert. The advantage to this is that it will substantially lessen the weight of the door, making it a lot easier to move around during the various phases of installation.

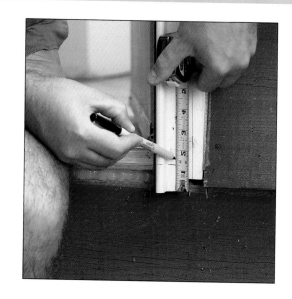

3 **Measure** With the door prepared, the next step is to choose which way the door will open—either hinged right or hinged left. Once you've decided, you can size the frame pieces to fit your door opening. To do this, start by positioning the hinge-side bar against the door frame opening on the hinge side you selected. Then mark where the bottom of the bar meets the threshold or sill. Next, use a tape measure to measure up from the bottom of the bar, *as shown,* so that you can transfer this measurement to the latch-side bar.

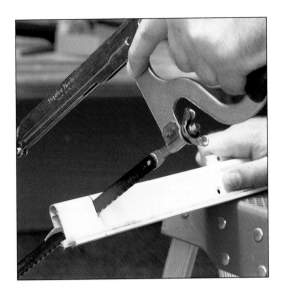

4 **Cut bars to length** After you've measured and marked both the hinge-side and latch-side bars, you can cut them to length. Support each piece firmly on a sawhorse or other sturdy work surface, and use a hacksaw fitted with a fine-tooth blade to cut each bar to length, *as shown in the photo at left.* When you're done with both, use a metal file to remove any sharp edges on the cut ends.

5 **Fasten hinged bar to door** Position the hinged bar on the edge of the door that you've selected to be the hinge side. Follow the manufacturer's instructions on how to position the bar on the door. Then use a ⅛" twist bit to drill through the center hole of each hinge and into the door. Install one of the screws provided in the hardware kit into each of the hinges to lock them in place. Then go back and drill the remaining hinge holes and drive in the remaining screws.

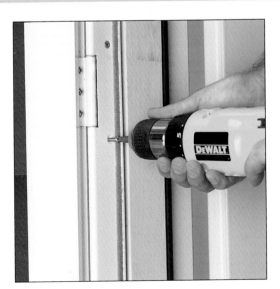

6 **Attach hinged door to jamb** Now you're ready to attach the storm door to the house. Start by lifting up the door and positioning it in the frame opening so that there's about a ¼" gap between the top of the frame opening and the top of the hinged door (this allows room for the top frame piece that's added later). When the hinge-side bar is snug against the jamb side of the molding, drive panhead screws through the predrilled holes in the face of the bar and into the front of the molding.

7 **Attach to front of jamb** Next, open the door and drive the panhead screws supplied by the manufacturer into the predrilled holes in the side of the bar. These screws are installed in the side of the exterior molding. Be careful not to overtighten any of these screws, as they have a tendency to strip easily. Repeat Steps 6 and 7 to install the latch-side bar and the header bar on top of the door frame.

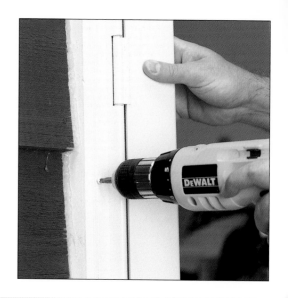

8 **Drill holes for latch** Since the storm door can hinge either way, the manufacturer can't install the latch in advance. In most cases, the latch hardware has its own set of installation instructions. Following these, measure up from the bottom of the door the recommended height and temporarily attach the supplied template to the latch side of the door. Then drill the suggested size holes in the door frame for the latch.

9 **Attach lever and latch** Insert one half of the door latch into the holes you just drilled in the door frame. Align the spindle that connects the operating mechanisms of both halves, and slide the two halves of the latch together. Then insert the mounting screws and tighten them to draw the halves together. Next, align the strike plate on the side jamb opposite the latch, and fasten it to the jamb with the screws provided (*see the photo at right*). Since the plate is slotted, you can move it up or down as needed for it to engage the latch properly.

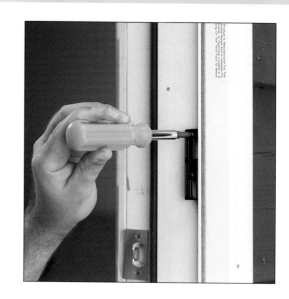

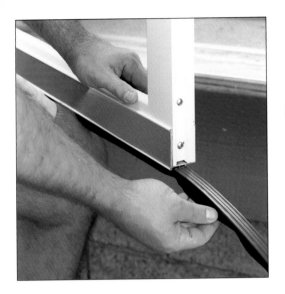

10 **Add the sweep** Most storm doors come with a bottom expander or sweep to compensate for any variations at the threshold and to create a watertight seal between the door and threshold. Open the door and slip the expander over the bottom of the door. Then carefully insert the rubber sweep into the channel in the bottom. Tip: To help the sweep slide in easily, apply a few drops of liquid detergent to the sweep before inserting it, to act as a lubricant. Push the sweep all the way in until it fully seats against the end of the channel.

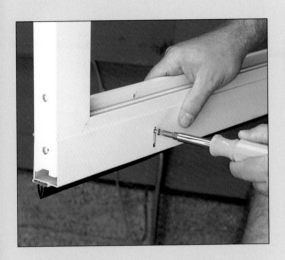

11 **Adjust the sweep** The bottom expander can be adjusted up or down to close any gaps at the bottom of the door. To do this, close the door and adjust the expander so that the sweep touches the threshold across the entire width of the door. With the expander in position, drill two pilot holes on the inside of the door through the expander and into the door. Then secure the expander to the door with the screws provided in the hardware kit (see the photo at left).

12 **Attach the screen** The final step is to select the appropriate insert for the season: either a glass pane or a screen. If the storm door you've installed has self-storing inserts, replace the glass pane you removed in Step 2 and position it as desired. For full-view storms like the one shown here, the inserts are held in place in the frame via a set of plastic snap-in retainer strips. Just position the desired insert and snap the strips in place.

Installing Door Trim

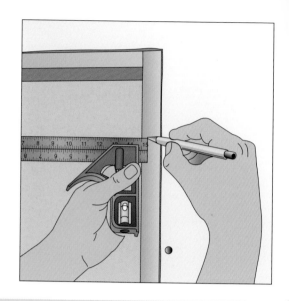

1 **Mark reveal** To install miter trim, start by marking the reveal on each jamb. A reveal is a slight offset between the trim and the jamb. It allows for easier installation and provides a shadow line for visual interest. The easiest way to mark this is to set the blade of a combination square so it protrudes ⅛". Then place a pencil against the blade of the square, press the head of the square against the jamb, and run these around the perimeter to mark the reveal.

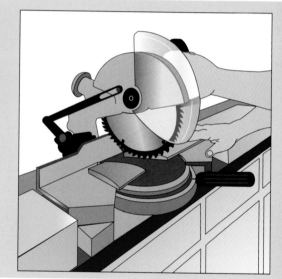

2 **Cut at miter** Once you've measured the trim pieces, you can cut them to length. My tool of choice here is a power miter saw, *like the one shown in the drawing at right.* A power miter saw cuts an accurate angle, and it's easy to adjust the angle slightly to compensate for out-of-square doors. If you've got a lot of trim to put up and you don't own one of these, consider renting one—it'll make the job a whole lot easier.

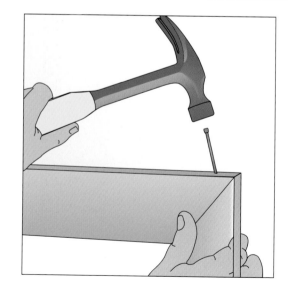

3 **Lock-nail** Once you've got the trim pieces cut to length, position each piece one at a time so the inside edge is flush with the marked reveal line. Nail the trim to the jamb with finish nails spaced about 12" apart. To close any gaps at the miter joints and to strengthen the joint, "lock-nail" the joints together *as shown in the drawing at right.* Here again, use a finish nail and make sure to stay away from the front edge, or else you'll split the trim piece.

A New Threshold

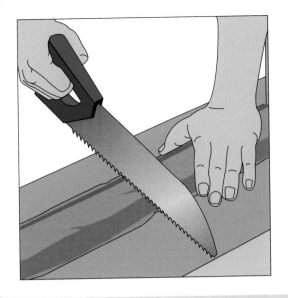

1 **Remove old threshold** To replace a worn-out threshold with a new one, start by removing the old threshold. If it's made of wood (*like the one shown here*), it's going to be nailed to the flooring. The simplest way to remove it is to cut it in half with a handsaw and then pry the halves up individually. Metal thresholds are typically screwed to the flooring. A rubber gasket often conceals these screws. Pry off the gasket to expose the screws, remove them with a screwdriver, and lift up the threshold to remove it.

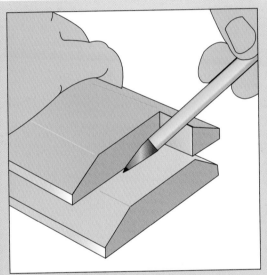

2 **Use old threshold as template** Most replacement thresholds will need to be trimmed to fit into the door opening and wrap around the doorjamb. The best way I've found to make sure the new threshold will fit perfectly is to use the old threshold as a template (assuming that it fit well in the first place). To do this, place the old threshold on top of the new one and trace the outline of the cutout. Cut wood thresholds with a handsaw or saber saw, and metal thresholds with a hacksaw.

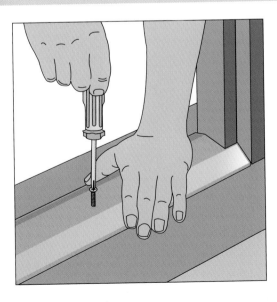

3 **Install new threshold** Check the fit of the new threshold, and use a wood or metal file to fine-tune it as necessary. Once you're satisfied with the fit, you can attach it to the flooring. Wood thresholds can be attached with screws or nails, and metal thresholds typically come with mounting screws in the package. If you're using screws, make sure to drill pilot holes and shank holes before driving in the screws.

Door Weatherstripping

Since many doors—especially solid-core wood doors—don't have tolerances that are as close as those manufactured into windows, they often don't achieve as tight a seal. This can result in considerable heating and cooling losses. The solution (outside of replacing the door with a high-quality door manufactured to tighter tolerances) is to add weatherstripping to create the seal. Weatherstripping for doors can be plastic or metal V-strips, open- or closed-cell foam, metal-reinforced felt or rubber gaskets, or a door sweep or door shoes that fit on the bottom of the door to create a seal at the threshold. For the most part, metal V-strips are your best bet—they create an excellent seal, stand up well to the elements, are easy to install, and are inexpensive. If you want to go with some type of gasket, avoid foam since it degrades rapidly; instead, go with reinforced felt or rubber gaskets—they'll hold up better in the long run.

V-channel Plastic or metal V-strips are an excellent way to help seal the gap between a door and jamb. Install self-adhesive plastic V-strips to a door so the V is pointing away from the door stop, *as shown in the photo at right.* Before you attach the strip, clean the doorjamb with a mild soap solution and let it dry thoroughly. Then peel the backing off the strip and press it into place. For added insurance against peeling, staple the strips to the jamb every 6" to 8".

Reinforced gasket Another type of weatherstripping that works well to seal gaps in doors is reinforced felt or rubber gaskets. Since most doors get a lot of use, the weatherstripping must be able to hold up well—that's why better-quality door weatherstripping is reinforced with a strip of metal. When fastened to the jamb with the nails provided by the manufacturer, the metal strip holds the gasket securely in place and protects it at the same time.

Foam strips Although foam strips are easy to apply, I don't generally recommend them for weatherstripping a door. In cases where the door isn't used much—such as the basement door *here*, which gets only occasional use—it'll work just fine. The problem with using a foam strip on a high-traffic door is that the foam quickly degrades because of exposure to the elements and the constant abrasion it receives. If you do decide to use self-adhesive foam, make sure to clean the surface well and let it dry before applying it.

ADDING A DOOR SHOE

One of the best ways to create a weathertight seal between the bottom of a door and its threshold is to add a door shoe. Door shoes come in a wide variety of styles, colors, and materials. Some are designed to slip over the base of a door and require little or no modification of the door itself (*like the one shown here*). Others require that you shorten the door to make room for the shoe. Whichever type you choose, make sure to follow the manufacturer's installation instructions.

Regardless of the type of shoe you choose, you'll most likely need to cut the shoe to length. Measure the door at

its bottom and transfer this measurement to the shoe. A hacksaw will cut through the shoe, whether it's plastic or metal (*see photo above*). Once the shoe is cut to length, slide it onto the bottom of the door (*see photo above right*). If the fit is snug, wipe a little liquid

detergent onto the sides of the shoe as a lubricant. With the shoe in place, drill pilot holes as instructed by the manufacturer, and fasten the shoe to the door with the screws provided.

Chapter 6

Window and Door Hardware

It's easy to overlook hardware when you're shopping for new windows and doors. That's because it's difficult enough just choosing the right style to blend in with your décor. But the hardware can play a major role in not only the visual impact of the window or door, but also how well it functions.

If you are planning on purchasing new or replacement windows and doors, make a concerted effort to inspect the hardware that comes with each unit (such as the sash locks on a window). And take your time selecting the hardware that doesn't come with the unit (such as the lockset for a door).

If you're not satisfied with the hardware that comes with the door or window, you can choose another brand, or if you really like the unit, you can upgrade the hardware yourself. This is also true for the existing window and door hardware in your home.

In this chapter, I'll start by showing you how to replace or install new sash locks (*opposite page*) and then move on to how to remove a lockset, including a nifty tip for preparing the door for a replacement set (*pages 98–99*). Next, I'll take you through the steps required to install a new

lockset—everything from installing the plunger mechanism to attaching the strike plate (*pages 100–101*).

If you need to install a lockset where there was none previously (such as when installing a new prehung door), I'll show you how to locate and drill the necessary holes for the lockset (*page 102*). There are also instructions on how to install or replace a security bolt in an exterior entry door (*page 103*). Security is also an issue with sliding patio doors, and I'll describe on *page 104* the most common ways to keep out intruders.

Finally, there are step-by step instructions on how to install a latch on a storm door (*page 105*), followed by details on what it takes to install and adjust an automatic door closer (*pages 106–107*).

Installing Sash Locks

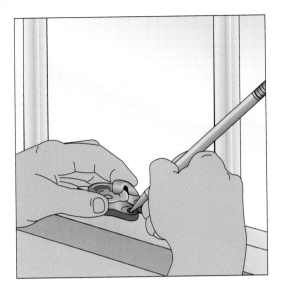

1 **Position the lock** Whether you're replacing a worn-out sash lock or installing a new one, the job is quick and easy. If you're replacing a sash lock, start by unscrewing the old one and removing it. To install a replacement or new lock, position both halves of the new sash lock so that each half rests on the appropriate sash and they're centered on the seam where the sashes meet. Odds are that you'll need to drill new holes for the mounting screws. Holding each half of the lock in position, make a mark through the mounting holes onto the sash.

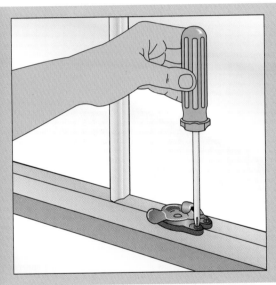

2 **Drill and secure** Remove both halves of the sash lock, and drill pilot holes for the mounting screws where you made marks in Step 1. Creating a small depression with an awl at each mark before drilling will provide the drill bit with an accurate starting point. After the holes are drilled, fasten each half of the lock to the sash with the mounting screws provided. Open and close the lock to make sure that it works properly and that it also pulls the sash firmly together when it's closed.

KEYED SASH LOCKS

If you can open and close sash locks only from the inside of your home, why would you want to install a keyed sash lock? Two reasons. First, some sash locks can be forced open from the outside by sliding a thin piece of stiff metal between the sashes – if the sash lock is keyed and locked, this can't happen.

Second, there are times where you may want to control access to a window from the inside. Keeping a curious child from experimenting with gravity (such as checking to see whether a cat really does land on all four feet when dropped out of a window) is a good example of this.

Removing a Lockset

1 **Remove knob** The first step in removing a lockset for replacement is to remove the interior knob or handle (as is the case *here*). Although it may seem that the knob or handle is held in place by some mysterious force, it's not. If you inspect the base of the knob or handle carefully, you'll find a small hole in it. To remove the knob or handle, all you have to do is insert an awl or nail through this hole and push in. This will release the catch that holds the knob or handle in place so that you can then pull it off.

2 **Remove cover plate** The next step is to remove the decorative cover plate, which conceals the retaining plate and retaining screws. Here again, this will appear to be held in place by magic. In this case, the cover plate is simply a press-fit over the retaining plate. To free it, first find the small notch in the rim of the plate. Then insert the tip of a flat-blade screwdriver in the notch and gently twist the screwdriver to force the cover plate away from the retaining plate.

3 **Remove retaining screws** Once the retaining plate is loose, pull it completely off and set it aside. At this point, the retaining screws that hold the two halves of the lockset together on the door should be exposed. Remove each of these screws with a screwdriver (they're usually quite long). Now you can pull the retaining plate out from the door and set it aside.

4 **Pull out the exterior knob** Once the retaining screws have been removed, you'll be able to remove the exterior knob or handle. Since this portion of the lockset usually has an extension that inserts into the plunger mechanism installed in the edge of the door, it might require a little wiggling to work it free. When the doorknob or handle is turned, it's the extension that causes the linkage in the plunger mechanism to retract the plunger. You can also persuade stubborn knobs to release their grip by tapping the extension gently with a hammer or mallet.

5 **Remove the plunger** The only remaining piece of lockset hardware to remove is the plumber mechanism. It's held in place in the edge of the door via a pair of mounting screws. After you've unscrewed these, you can pull out the plunger mechanism. This is often a tight fit and will also need some persuasion to come out. The simplest way to do this is to insert a screwdriver into the opening in the plunger mechanism for the extension of the exterior knob. Then strike the shaft of the screwdriver from the side to force the plunger mechanism out.

TOOTHPICK TIP

If you've removed the lockset to replace it with a new one, you may find that the plunger mechanism of the new lockset fits into the mortise (the shallow rectangular recess) in the edge of the door. This is good because it will save you the work of chopping a new mortise. In many cases, even the mounting holes in the new plunger mechanism will line up with the old screw holes. In order to provide sufficient purchase for the new mounting screws, try this simple trick: Insert a toothpick or sliver of wood (*as shown here*) into the mounting holes before driving in the screws to give the screws something to "bite" into.

Installing a New Lockset

How difficult or easy it is to install a new lockset will depend on a couple of things. First, if you're simply replacing an old lockset and the new unit is sized the same, it's really a matter of reversing the order of disassembly to install the new unit (*see pages 98–99*). As long as the hole sizes are the same, most new locksets allow you to adjust the length of the plunger to compensate for differences in the offset—that is, the distance the large hole is from the edge of the door. If you insert the plunger and find that the stem holes (the holes through which the mounting screws pass) are centered in the hole, the plunger needs no adjustment. In many cases, you'll either need to enlarge the mortise in the door edge for the plunger face plate, or cut one to fit if you're installing a lockset in a new door. In either case, just push the plunger in until the face plate butts up against the edge and trace around it with a pencil. Then remove about ⅛" of material inside the marked lines with a sharp chisel.

1 **Secure plunger** Once the mortise in the door edge has been cut or trimmed to accept the plunger face plate, check the fit by pressing the plunger mechanism all the way in. If the fit is good, drill two pilot holes to accept the mounting screws, and install these with a screwdriver. Note: If you're replacing a lockset and will be using the existing holes, *see the sidebar on page 99* for a tip to help the new screws grip better.

2 **Attach first half** Now that the plunger mechanism is in place, you can begin installing the two halves of the lockset. Start by inserting the half that contains the long extension that passes through the plunger mechanism. In most cases, this extension is keyed to fit only one way. Insert the tip of the extension in the hole in the plunger mechanism, and push the knob in until it butts up against the face of the door. Check the operation now by turning the handle—the plunger in the edge of the door should go smoothly in and out as you turn.

3 **Insert second half** Now you can install the second half of the lockset. Here again, the cavity inside the knob or handle will be keyed to slip over the extension only one way. Align the cavity with the extension, and push the knob onto it until it butts up against the face of the door. Once again, check the operation from this side by twisting the knob to make sure the plunger retracts and extends smoothly.

4 **Secure halves together** All that's left on the lockset is to secure the two halves together. Depending on the type of lockset, the retaining screws that hold the parts together may or may not be concealed after they're installed with a cover plate. On the inexpensive lockset *shown here*, these screws are left exposed. Insert the screws in the holes in the knob or retaining plate so that they pass through the stem holes in the plunger and into the second half of the lockset. Tighten them with a screwdriver, and check the operation of the plunger.

5 **Add strike plate** With the lockset in place, you can install the strike plate in the door jamb. For a replacement lockset, position the new strike plate where the existing one was. To locate a strike plate on a new door, try this simple trick. Rub a little lipstick or crayon on the plunger, then close the door. The lipstick will leave a mark on the door jamb exactly where you'll need to locate the strike plate. If necessary, drill a clearance hole for the plunger. Then drill pilot holes for the strike plate and secure it with the screws provided.

New Holes for a Lockset

1 **Measure up** Drilling holes for a new lockset has been greatly simplified since lockset manufacturers started including templates in their lockset installation instructions. These paper templates are designed to fold over the edge of the door to precisely locate the center-points of the holes for drilling. Before you can use a template, however, you'll need to determine where on the door you want the lockset. The recommended centerline for most doors is 36" up from the bottom of the door.

2 **Position template** Once you've marked the center-line on the door, fold the template, following the manufacturer's directions to select the desired offset (the distance from the center of the hole to the edge of the door). Position the template on the door so that its centerline is aligned with the mark you made in Step 1. Then fasten the template to the door with masking tape. Note: In most cases, the template will also locate the center-point of the hole in the edge of the door for the plunger mechanism. Drill the large diameter first, then the plunger hole, using the appropriate bits (*see the sidebar below*).

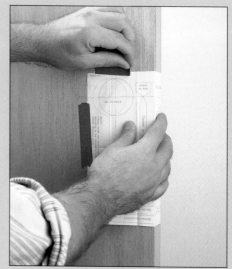

INSTALLATION KITS

To make installing a lockset as simple as possible, many tool accessory manufacturers offer lockset installation kits, like the one *shown here*. These kits typically consist of a hole saw and a spade bit. It's important to note that you'll need to match the installation kit to the lockset you've purchased. This is easy, since all lockset makers list the recommended drill sizes right on their packaging. Note that the rim of the hole saw is intentionally short—you can't drill all the way through the door in one pass. Instead, you have to drill from both sides. This prevents splintering and leaves a clean hole.

Installing a Security Bolt

1 **Use template** There are a couple different types of security locks that you can install on any door. One style is a rim-lock cylinder that features vertical deadbolts; the other is a horizontal cylinder that offers a lower profile (*shown here*). Whichever type you use, the first thing to do is locate where you want to install the lock. Most security locks are installed 6" to 8" above the lockset. Make a mark and then fold the template. Align it with the mark you made on the door, and tape it in place.

2 **Drill with hole saw** Although you can drill directly through the template (*as shown here*), it's also a good idea to first mark the centerpoint of the holes you need to drill, using an awl, in case the paper rips as you begin drilling. Drill the large hole first with the appropriate-sized hole saw. Do not drill all the way through in one pass, or you'll splinter the opposite face of the door as the bit exits. Instead, drill in from both sides. Next, use a spade bit to drill the hole for the plunger mechanism (*inset*).

3 **Install the lock** Install the security bolt, beginning with the plunger mechanism, by pressing it in until it butts against the edge of the door. Then trace around the face plate, remove it, and chisel out a ⅛"-deep depression. Reinsert the mechanism and secure it with the screws provided. Next, insert the half of the lock with the extension into the large hole and feed the extension through the hole in the plunger mechanism. Insert the extension into the cavity in the remaining half and fasten the halves together. Finally, install the strike plate in the doorjamb, following the manufacturer's directions.

Sliding-Door Security

Although sliding doors do offer easy access to decks, porches, and patios along with great views, the one thing they don't offer is very good security. That's because the latches of most sliding panels are held in place with only a couple of screws. All it takes to rip these out of a doorjamb is a determined intruder. To make it even easier to do this, there's a handle on the exterior of the door that affords an intruder a good grip. Alternatively they can use a pry bar— a quick twist is all it takes to get instant access to your home. To prevent this from happening, many homeowners fortify the security of their sliding doors with some form of security bar that prevents the sliding panel from being forced open; *see below*. Another option is to add vertical deadbolts to the sliding panel. Although these do add extra security, they can still be ripped out with a pry bar.

Commercial security bars Most of the metal security bars available are adjustable to fit either 5-foot- or 6-foot-wide patio doors. The security bar *shown here* mounts to the middle of the doorjamb by way of a bracket that allows the bar to pivot down out of the way when not in use. The other end of the bar engages a U-shaped bracket attached to the sliding door panel. **Caution:** Before you install the bracket on the sliding panel, check with the door manufacturer to make sure you won't damage the panes or the seal when drilling the pilot holes for the bracket.

Shop-made security bars It's not as fancy as the metal version *shown above,* but a good ol' 2×4 cut to fit between the sliding panel and the doorjamb does the same job. The only disadvantage to this is that you have to remember to remove it when you go to open the door. This might sound silly, but because it's on the floor. it's easy to miss. And as there will always be a bit of clearance between the 2×4 and the sliding panel, you'll be able to open it just enough to slam into it. Beside being annoying, this isn't good for the long-term health of the door.

Installing a Storm Door Latch

1 **Install latch** A storm door latch is simple to install because the plunger is external instead of being encased in the door. If you're replacing a latch, remove the two mounting screws, *as shown in the drawing,* and pull the two halves out from the door. If the replacement latch is similar in size, simply insert the two halves and fasten them together. To install a new latch, drill holes for the extension that connects the two parts and for the mounting screws; *see Step 8 on page 90 for more on this.*

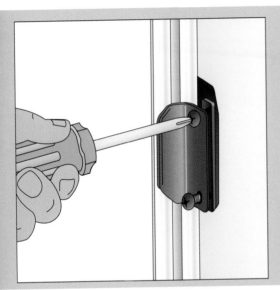

2 **Attach strike plate** The plunger on a typical storm door engages a strike plate attached to the door-jamb. Since both parts are exposed when the door is closed (versus concealed when a door is closed with a lock-set plunger), it's easy to locate the strike plate. With the storm door closed, position the strike plate so it engages the plunger. Then mark through the mounting holes in the strike plate and drill pilot holes. Fasten the strike plate to the jamb with the screws provided.

3 **Shim or adjust as necessary** As is often the case, the doorjamb may be too far away from the plunger in the door latch to engage properly. Most storm door latch manufacturers supply precut plastic shims to insert behind the strike plate to bring the strike plate out far enough to engage the plunger. To install the shims, remove the strike plate mounting screws and insert the shims behind the plate. Reinstall the screws and check for proper operation. Add or remove shims as necessary until the plunger engages smoothly without sticking.

Door Closers

1 **Locate the closer** Although door closers are usually installed on storm doors (*as shown here*), they can be used to close almost any door. Heavy-duty closers are available that can handle even a solid-core door. Regardless of the type you install, the first step is to locate the jamb bracket. Most brackets are fastened to the door frame at the desired height approximately ¼" away from the door (check the installation directions). If more latching force is desired, you can usually move the bracket up to 1" away from the door (note that this also reduces how far the door opens).

2 **Attach the closer** Next, slide the hold-open washer onto the rod. Now you can attach the closer to the jamb bracket. These two parts are typically held together with a small connecting pin that passes through a hole in the jamb bracket and a hole in the end of the rod. Move the hold-open washer over the lugs in the rod to properly tension the rod for installation. Don't move this until after the installation is complete.

3 **Locate bracket** Once the closer is attached to the jamb bracket, you can locate where the door bracket will be installed on the door frame. Attach the door bracket to the closer with the connecting pin provided. Here again, the pin will pass through a hole in the front bracket and a hole in the closer rod. With the door tightly closed, position the door bracket on the door frame so that the closer is level, and mark the locations for the two mounting holes.

4 **Drill holes** Pivot the closer out of the way, and then use a centerpunch or awl to make a depression in the door frame to help start the drill bit. Next, drill two pilot holes for the mounting screws with the bit recommended by the manufacturer. **Caution:** Take care not to drill through the door. The simplest way to prevent this is to apply a piece of masking tape about ½" up from the end of the drill bit to serve as an indicator of when to stop drilling. Make sure the bit is sharp, and use minimal pressure to prevent from drilling into the opposite side once you break through the surface that you're drilling through.

5 **Attach bracket** Now you can attach the door bracket to the door with the screws provided in the hardware kit. As you drive these in, be careful not to overtighten them. If the door frame is vinyl or metal, the screws can easily strip. Wood frames hold screws better but can still strip the screws if too much force is used. With the closer installed, open the door and move the hold-open washer behind the lugs on the closer rod.

6 **Adjust tension** In most cases, you'll need to adjust the tension on the closer rod to control both how quickly the door closes and how hard or soft the door frame comes to a complete stop against the doorjamb. The speed with which the closer operates is controlled by way of an adjustment screw on one end of the closer cylinder. A little trial and error adjusting is all it takes to get the desired speed.

Chapter 7

Repair and Maintenance

It seems to me sometimes that we've all been conditioned to live with doors and windows that stick, bind, and just don't operate correctly. I think it has to do with the fact that most of us grew up with solid-wood windows and doors. Many of these older units weren't very well made and didn't stand up well to constant use and to the never-ending battle against the elements. Over time, we just got used to them not working—it was a part of life to prop open a window with a piece of wood, or kick a door in that special spot to get it to open.

Well, it doesn't have to be that way. Most door and window repairs are simple and straightforward. The first thing we have to do is acknowledge the problem so that we can fix it, instead of living with it or ignoring it. In this chapter, I'll show you how to repair and maintain the windows and doors in your home. No longer will you have to press down on a doorknob to allow the door to swing open or live with a window that won't stay open or closed.

I'll start by showing you a couple of ways to free a stuck window (*opposite page*), then I'll describe how to lubricate a window for smooth operation, including which type of lubricant you should use and, just as important, which type of lubricant you shouldn't use (*page 110*).

In case the windows in your house use spiral balances to operate, I've included a section on how to adjust them using a specialty tool (*page 111*). Next, I'll go over how to replace an operating mechanism in an awning or casement window (*pages 112–113*). This is the mechanism that forces the window sash open or closed and that, because it's used so often, will eventually wear out. If you live in a temperate region and have jalousie windows (*see page 11*), I'll show you how to replace the operating mechanism and replace a broken or chipped louver (*pages 114–115*).

Then there are step-by-step instructions on how to repair two common problems: damaged screens and broken windows—everything from installing rubber spline in screens to reglazing a glass window (*pages 116–119*). I've also included directions on how to cut your own glass (*page 120*). Finally, some door repairs, beginning with dealing with sticking doors (*pages 121–123*) and finishing with how to repair a hollow-core door (*pages 124–125*).

Freeing a Stuck Window

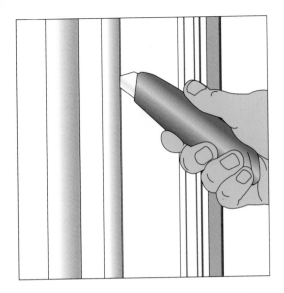

Utility knife In situations where a window has been freshly painted, the newest layer of paint can form a bond between the window jamb and the sash. Quite often, all that it takes to free the window is to run a utility knife between the jamb and the sash to sever this bond—usually between the parting stop and sash, *as shown*. Take care to guide the knife with a firm grip and go slowly. If you go fast, the tip of the blade can "catch" and follow the grain, veering off course and leaving a deep scratch.

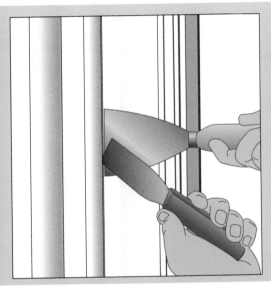

Two putty knives Occasionally, paint can seep in behind the sash and create an even stronger bond between the jamb and the sash. In cases like this, it's necessary to apply some force to break the bond. The least destructive way to do this is to use two stiff-blade putty knives: one to protect the jamb, and another to serve as a lever to free the sash. The easiest way to insert either knife is to press it in at an angle, *as shown*. It's also a good idea to file a slight bevel on the edge to help it slip in.

PAINT ZIPPER

If you've got a house full of older wood double-hung windows, you'll find this nifty gadget particularly useful. It's called a paint zipper, a window zipper, or sash zipper, and it's used to free stuck windows. Serrated edges on the tip of the blade allow you to literally saw away old paint and gunk trapped between the sash and the jamb. Sharp points on the end of the blade are great for getting into corners and freeing stuck parts. Paint zippers cost around $6 and can be found in most hardware stores and specialty paint shops.

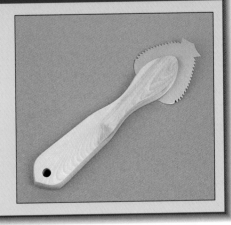

Lubricating a Window

Since almost all windows have moving parts, they will benefit from occasional lubrication. The type of lubrication you'll use to help the sash move smoothly up and down or in and out will depend on what it's made of: wood, metal, or vinyl (*see the sections below*). But the sash isn't the only part of a window that needs lubrication. Sash locks, operating mechanisms, and spring-loaded storm window locks all need regular maintenance. Virtually all the parts listed above will work better, last longer, and stay rust-free with a once- or twice-a-year spray of a petroleum-based lubricant like WD-40. When using this, take care to concentrate the spray on moving parts only, and always wipe off any excess spray—almost all lubricants will attract dust and will eventually form into a gooey mess.

Paraffin on wood Call me old-fashioned, but I still feel that paraffin is the best lubricant to use for a wooden sash. Not only does it keep that sash running smoothly, it also helps protect the finish. To apply paraffin, start by cleaning the jamb with a mild detergent solution. After it has dried, gently rub a piece of paraffin (you'll find it at most hardware stores, or in grocery stores where the canning supplies are located) in the groove where the sash operates. Then check the operation and apply more if necessary.

Silicone on vinyl or metal The sashes on most metal and vinyl windows don't usually require lubrication to operate smoothly. But if you do notice a sash sticking, try spraying on a very light coat of silicone spray to the sash channel. An alternative to this is to spray some silicone on a clean, dry cloth and use this to apply it to the channel. This second method reduces overspray and concentrates the lubricant exactly where it's needed. Apply a small amount at a time and check the operation. Repeat until it works smoothly.

Adjusting a Spiral Balance

1 **Tilt sash in** If your windows use a spiral balance mechanism to operate the sash and you notice that the sash doesn't stay open all the way—it slides back down a bit after you let it go—or it doesn't close properly, the spiral balance needs to be adjusted. To do this, you'll need a spiral balance adjusting tool. You can usually buy one of these from a window contractor. In order to use the tool, you need to access the spring. Depress the locking tabs on the top of the sash and tilt it in *as shown*.

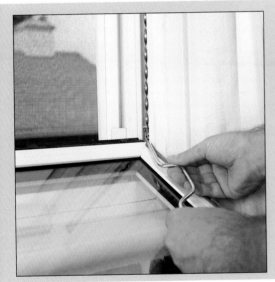

2 **Unhook the spiral balance** The next step is to unhook the spiral balance from the double-pronged bracket that holds it in place against the jamb. The tip of the spiral balance adjusting tool is designed to hook over the pin in the bottom of the spring. Be aware that this spring is under tension and will unwind if you accidentally let go of the end. This isn't the end of the world, however; it just means that it'll take you longer to get the spring adjusted correctly.

3 **Adjust the tension** You'll notice that the tool is shaped to make it easy to wind in either direction: clockwise to increase tension, counterclockwise to decrease it. It's important to try to match the tension of the two springs; otherwise one side will have to work harder than the other. As you increase or decrease tension, count the number of turns you make so that you can do the same for the opposite spring. In either case, adjust in small steps, one or two turns at a time. Pull the spring down with the tool and hook it back onto the bracket. Check to see whether it operates smoothly, and repeat if needed.

Replacing an Awning Mechanism

Awning and casement windows use a special operating mechanism to force the window sash open or closed. Because these scissors-like mechanisms get a lot of use and often have to move heavy sashes, they will eventually fail. Pins will shear off, brackets can bend or break, and parts can rub together, causing binding. Although these pages show how to replace the operating mechanism on an awning window, the steps are virtually identical for replacing a casement mechanism; the only difference is that instead of the mechanism being on the bottom of the window, a casement mechanism is located on the side. Replacing the mechanism is fairly straightforward. The challenge is getting a replacement. Unfortunately, operating mechanisms vary considerably, so your best bet is to remove the old one and take it to a home center or window specialist to get an exact replacement.

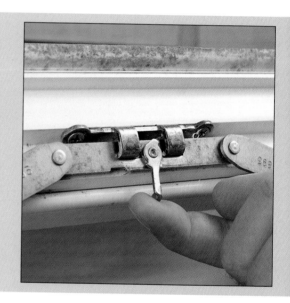

1 **Toggle the latch** The first step in removing an operating mechanism for an awning or casement window is to unhook the mechanism from the sash itself. This allows you to move it out of the way to provide better access to the mechanism. In most cases, the operating mechanism attaches to the sash by way of a bracket with a set of tabs that hook into the mechanism. The mechanism is held in place on the bracket with a small latch. To release it, pivot the latch open with your finger, *as shown*.

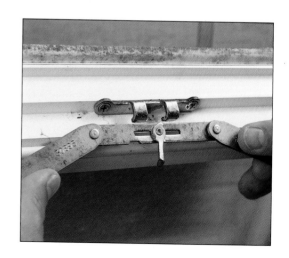

2 **Disconnect mechanism from sash** Once the latch is released, you can disconnect the end of the operating mechanism from the sash. Although this sounds simple, it can be a bit tricky. That's because the length of the tabs can vary considerably among manufacturers. Short tabs are simple: Just press down slightly on the end of the mechanism to release them. Longer tabs often require considerable pressure to force the bracket down far enough that it will clear the tabs.

3 **Remove mounting screws** The next step is to remove the mounting screws that secure the operating mechanism to the window jamb. On most windows, you'll find that you'll have better access to these screws by splaying the legs of the bracket open *as shown.* You'll also find that it's easier to remove the screws on the outside of the window instead of trying to unscrew them from the inside. Make sure to set these screws aside in case the new mechanism doesn't include these in its kit.

4 **Pull out the mechanism** With the mechanism free from the window jamb, you can remove it. Start by pressing the legs of the mechanism closed (as if the window were fully open). This will allow you to pull the mechanism out and thread the legs through the small slot in the bottom of the window jamb. After you've removed the mechanism, clean the jamb with a mild detergent solution and let it dry before installing the new operating mechanism.

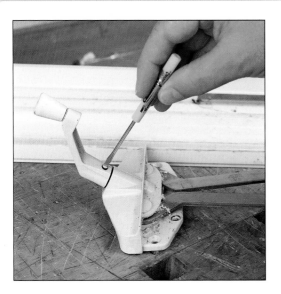

5 **Remove the knob** Many replacement mechanisms do not come with an operating knob. So make sure to remove the knob from the old mechanism before you discard it. Operating knobs are typically held in place by a small setscrew on the underside of the knob. To install the new mechanism, simply reverse the steps you took to disassemble and remove the old mechanism. Note: If the new mechanism isn't prelubricated, spray on a light coat of petroleum-based spray to all linkages and pivot points to keep it running smoothly.

Repairing Jalousie Windows

Of all the windows that can be installed in a home, a jalousie window has the most moving parts. That's because each of the individual glass slats pivots on its own. Fortunately, the operating mechanism that makes this all happen is fairly simple. Each glass slat is held in place with a pair of brackets. These brackets have two holes for rivets that serve as pivot points. The hole in the body of the bracket attaches to the window frame. The other hole is located in an arm underneath the bracket and attaches to an operating rod that's connected to the operating mechanism. Turning the knob on the operating mechanism forces the operating rod to move up or down, which in turn causes the brackets holding the glass slats to pivot open or closed. Since this operating mechanism is moving a lot of linkages and heavy glass, it's prone to wear and tear. Here again, replacement is simple; finding the replacement mechanism is the challenge—consult a local window specialist for parts.

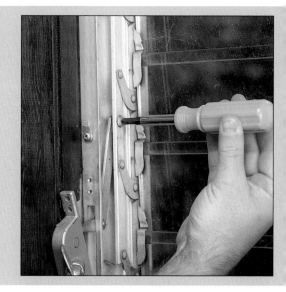

1 **Remove operating rod screws** To replace a worn-out or broken operating mechanism, start by removing the screws that connect the arm of the mechanism to the operating rod, *as shown.* On cheaper jalousie windows, you may find that the arm is connected to the operating mechanism with rivets. If this is the case, you'll need to drill out the rivets with a power drill and a twist bit. Then when you replace the mechanism, you'll have to attach the arm with blind or "Pop" rivets.

2 **Remove mounting screws** After you've detached the arm of the operating mechanism from the operating rod, the next step is to remove the mounting screws that secure the operating mechanism to the window frame, *as shown.* Here again, it's a good idea to set these screws aside in a safe place because the new mechanism may or may not come with replacement screws.

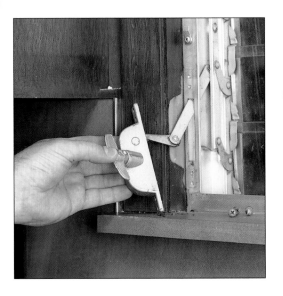

3 **Pull out the mechanism** All that's left is to carefully remove the operating mechanism from the window frame *as shown.* As you pull it out, take care to thread the connecting arm out of the slot so that it doesn't damage the slot. After you've removed the mechanism, clean the area with a mild detergent solution and then let it dry. To install the new mechanism, just reverse the steps you took to remove the old one.

REPLACING BROKEN OR DAMAGED SLATS

Just like any glass window, the slat in a jalousie window can chip or break. The nice thing about this is that you have to replace only the damaged slat, not an entire pane. Most home centers and some hardware stores stock slats for jalousie windows and will cut them to length for you. Note that this is not ordinary glass, as the front edges are rounded over to prevent cuts and scratches—make sure you use this type of glass and not regular glass, to prevent future injuries.

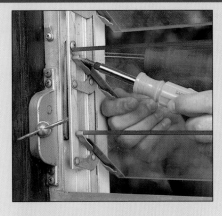

Bend Tabs To remove a glass slat, pry the lipped end of the bracket up with a screwdriver, *as shown.* Take care to pry just enough to slide the slat out—if you pry too much, you can break the bracket. Use gentle pressure here and take your time. Free both ends of the slat before proceeding.

Pull Out After you've freed both ends of the slat, gently slide out each end, working back and forth between the ends, sliding each about 1/2" as you go. Slow down as the last of the slats slips out from under the bracket, to prevent the lipped edge from shearing off a glass fragment from the edge of the slat. Reverse the process to install the new slat.

Repairing Window Screens

1 **Remove spline and screen** To repair damaged screening on a metal or vinyl window, start by removing the rubber spline that holds the screening in place. (For repairing screening on a wood window, *see the opposite page.*) The rubber spline fits in a groove in the frame and pinches the screening in place. To remove it, find the end (usually at a corner) and pry it up with an awl or other pointed tool. Then grab the lifted end and pull up to remove the spline and lift out the damaged screen.

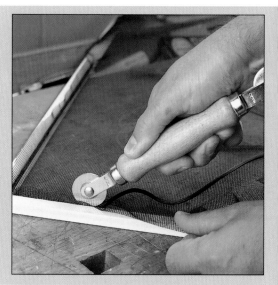

2 **Install new screening** The new screening you install can be either fiberglass (*as shown here*) or aluminum. Both can be cut to fit with a sharp utility knife or scissors. Measure the frame and add a couple of inches to both the width and the length. Place the screening centered on the frame and begin inserting the rubber spline, starting at one corner. A special splining tool that looks like a double-ended pizza cutter makes this easy. One wheel is concave and is used to press in the spline; the other end is convex and can be used to preform aluminum screening into the groove so that it's easier to insert the spline.

3 **Trim away excess** After you've inserted the spline all the way around the frame, you can trim away the excess screening. The best tool for the job is a utility knife with a fresh blade. Make sure to hold the knife so that the cutting edge runs slightly above the spline, and then gently move the blade along the frame *as shown.* Go slowly here to prevent the blade from accidentally hopping off the frame and into the screening—it would be a shame to have to replace the screening that you just installed.

4 **Wood screens: Remove old trim** The screening on wood screens (typically aluminum) is held in place with staples. To get to these staples, you'll first have to remove the wood trim, or screen molding, that covers them. This molding is primarily there to conceal the rough edges of the screen while also covering the staples. To remove the screen molding, start by running the tip of a utility knife between the molding and the frame to break the paint bond. Then use a stiff putty knife to pry up the molding. Set aside the molding—you'll replace it after you've installed the new screening.

5 **Wood screens: Remove staples** Now that the staples are exposed, you can remove them with a flat-blade screwdriver or a pair of needlenose pliers. Lift off the old screening and cut a new piece to fit; if possible, use the old screening as a pattern. Center the new screening on the frame and attach it with staples (a staple gun works best for this). Next, remove the old nails in the screen molding by pulling them out from behind with a pair of pliers and then attach them to the frame with brads. Countersink the holes with a nail set, and fill them with exterior-grade putty.

SCREEN KITS

Occasionally, the frame on a screen will get damaged and need to be replaced. Most homeowners will take the screen in to the local hardware store for repair. In most cases, the hardware store will throw out the old screen and make a new one. Instead of paying them to do this, you can do it yourself with one of the easy-to-use screen kits that are available at most home centers (*see the photo at right*). A screen kit consists of four frame pieces that you can cut to length, corner brackets that connect the pieces, and screening and splining: everything you need to build a new screen—at about half the cost.

Repairing a Broken Window

1 **Remove glass fragments** Whenever you need to repair a broken window, it's always a lot easier to do the job if you can remove the sash from the window frame to make the repair. Unfortunately, sometimes this is either inconvenient or impossible. To repair a broken window, start by removing the glass fragments. Slip on a pair of leather gloves to protect your hands, carefully remove any loose pieces, and set them aside.

2 **Remove trim or glazing compound** Depending on how the windowpane is held in place, you'll need to either remove trim pieces (*as shown here*) or remove the existing glazing compound. A stiff putty knife or an old chisel and a lot of elbow grease are required to remove this stubborn material. You may find it easier to remove the putty if you apply some heat with a heat gun. The heat softens up the putty and allows you to get under it with a knife. It's important to remove all of it—even a small lump can cause the new glass to fracture while it's being installed.

3 **Prepare the bed** To provide a cushion between the new glass pane and the wood, metal, or vinyl frame, a bed of glazing compound or putty is applied to the frame. Before you apply the glazing compound, clean the frame with mineral spirits to ensure a good bond. There are a couple of ways to prepare the bed. One way is to scoop out a dollop of glazing compound and roll it into a thin coil; then press the coil into the frame. The method I prefer is to press a bed of compound into the frame with a putty knife; *see the photo at right.*

4 **Install new pane** With the bed prepared, the next step is to install the new glass pane. You can either cut the glass to fit yourself (*see page 120 for step-by-step directions on how to do this*) or have it cut for you at your local glass shop, hardware store, or home center. Make sure to measure carefully, and cut or have the glass cut ⅛" narrower and shorter than the width and height to allow room for the frame pieces to expand and contract. Press the pane gently into the bed of glazing compound so that it compresses the bed slightly.

5 **Install glazier's points** Although most folks think that glass panes are held in place by the glazing compound, they're really locked into the frame with small metal clips call glazier's points (*inset*). The clips butt up against the glass and are forced into the frame or trim pieces to secure the glass. To make it easier to insert these metal clips, some manufacturers have designed clips that use a special installation tool, like the one *shown here.* Take care not to apply any sideways pressure—use only downward pressure—since it's surprisingly easy to fracture the glass.

6 **Apply new glazing compound** Now that the pane is locked securely in the frame, you can apply new glazing compound or install the molding or trim you removed in Step 2. Here again, you can apply the compound by first rolling a coil and pressing it in place or else apply it directly to the frame with a putty knife (*as shown here*). Once you're done, use a moistened fingertip to smooth the glazing compound to create a gentle slope that will help shed water from the frame.

CUTTING GLASS

1 **Score the glass** All it takes to cut your own glass to size is a piece of glass, a flat surface, leather gloves, and a glass cutter. Start by laying the glass to be cut on a flat surface, protected with a layer of newspaper (or a rubber router mat, *as shown here*). Using a straight-edge as a guide, run the glass cutter along the surface of the glass to score it. Since cutters cost only a few bucks, make sure you use a new one with a sharp cutting wheel. Gentle pressure on the wheel is all that's required. Some folks like to dip the wheel in kerosene as a lubricant, but I've never found this to be necessary if the wheel is sharp.

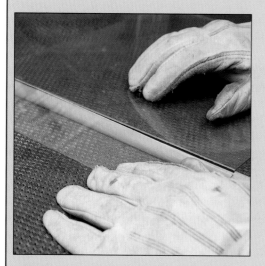

2 **Snap the glass** Once the glass is scored, it can be separated by snapping it in two. The best way I've found to do this is to slip a length of dowel directly under the scored line and then press down on both sides of the glass *as shown.* Make sure to wear leather gloves here and apply only gentle pressure—you'll be surprised how easily it snaps. I don't recommend snapping the glass on the edge of a bench or other work surface—the glass can slip out of your hands and shatter on the floor.

3 **Snapping strips** Occasionally, you'll find that you need to trim just a narrow strip off a piece of glass. Although scoring it isn't a problem, snapping it off accurately can be a challenge. Here's a nifty tip that will allow you to precisely snap off a narrow strip. Just cut a long slot or kerf in the edge of a scrap of wood (a table saw works best for this). Then slip the kerf over the strip so the edge of the scrap piece aligns with the line you scored. Give the scrap piece a twist of your wrist, and the narrow strip will snap off cleanly.

Dealing with Sticking Doors

Causes of binding Why is it that we so often ignore a binding door, hoping the problem will go away when the season changes? In cases of solid-wood doors, this may in fact occur, since the wood swells or shrinks as it reacts to changes in humidity—moist in the summer and dry in the winter. Even if it does go away eventually, why live with it? A sticking or binding door is usually quite easy to fix.

A sticking door can be caused by a number of problems. The solution to the problem depends on where the door sticks. If the entire edge of a door rubs up against the jamb (A), you'll need to either plane the full length of the door's edge (*see page 123*) or deepen all of the hinge mortises.

If the latch edge of a door rubs just at the top or bottom (B or C), deepen the corresponding hinge mortise. If the top or bottom edge of the door binds (D or E), you can solve the problem by either shimming the appropriate hinge (*see page 122*) or planing off the offending area. For doors that bind at the latch plate area (F), simply deepen the mortise for the strike plate.

Check for clearance In addition to the causes of binding described *above*, there's another place where a door can bind: If the door stops are set in too close to the door, the door will rub up against them, causing problems. The most typical of these is that the door won't want to close fully, or it won't stay closed. To check to make sure you've got sufficient clearance between the stops and the door, check it with a playing card *as shown*. You should be able to slide the card between them over the full length of the door. If you can't, remove the stops and reinstall them.

Making a shim Shims can solve a surprising number of binding problems without the hassle of removing the door. To make a full-sized shim for a hinge, start by removing the hinge screws. Then insert a piece of stiff paper (a business card or index card works well) behind the hinge and mark the width, the length, and the hole locations. Now cut the shim to size with scissors or a utility knife—I like to make a half-dozen or so at a time. Cut out square holes for the hinge screws with a utility knife as well.

Inserting shim behind hinge To remove binding on the bottom edge of the latch side, insert a shim or two behind the top hinge (*as shown*). For binding at the top edge, insert a shim or two behind the bottom hinge. Drive the hinge screws back in and check the operation. Basically what shimming does is tilts the door just a bit. Be aware that too many shims can actually causing binding, opposite the hinge you're shimming.

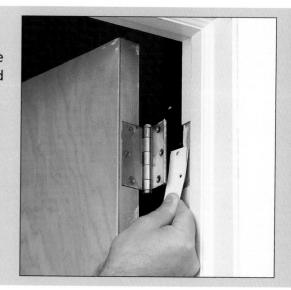

Partial shims If you don't want to hassle with removing hinges and cutting shims to size, you can sometimes get away with using a partial shim. Here's how to install one. Start by loosening the hinge-mounting screws, but don't remove them. Then cut a piece of index card to length and width so that you can fold it in half lengthwise and insert it behind the hinge. Tighten the hinge screws and check the operation. Repeat as necessary to eliminate the binding.

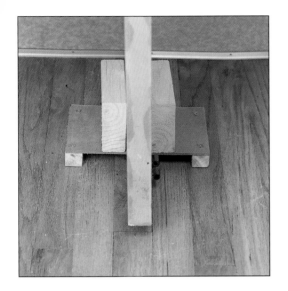

Door jacks In some situations you'll just have to give in and plane the edge of a door. The challenge to this is holding the darn thing upright so that you can plane, file, or sand off the problem area. Here's where some simple shop-made "door jacks" can come to the rescue; *see the sidebar below.* To use the jacks, slip a jack under each end of the door. The weight of the door will cause the plywood to bow and firmly grip the door frame so that you can plane it.

Planing a door The type of plane you use will depend on how much stock needs to be removed and where it is. For small jobs, and when planing end grain, I like to use a block plane (*see the photo at left*). Its low-angle blade can handle end grain, and it will quickly level any high spots. If you need to plane the entire edge of a door, I suggest a jack plane or jointer plane. Their longer bodies allow you to knock off the high spots that a shorter block plane would simply follow. If you're not into hand tools, a belt sander also works well; just make sure to keep it moving to prevent it from digging in.

SHOP-MADE DOOR JACKS

Propping up a door so that you can work on it is easy with these shop-made door jacks. To make a set, glue and screw 2×4 scraps to a piece of ½"-thick plywood; *see the drawing at right.* Don't be tempted to use thicker plywood thinking that it'll be better. You *want* the plywood to bow so that the 2×4 scraps will bow in and grip the door. Use the thickness of the door to size the gap between the 2×4 scraps mounted to the top of the plywood (it should be around 1½" to 1⅝" thick).

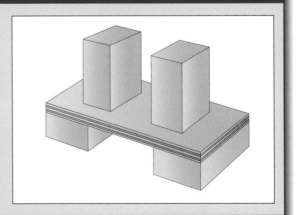

Repairing a Hollow-Core Door

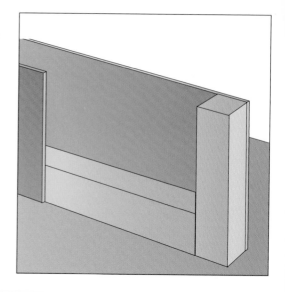

In order to repair a hollow-core door, you have to know what's inside it. Basically, a hollow-core door is made by covering a wood frame with two sheets or "skins" of wood veneer—typically lauan, birch, or oak (*see the drawing at right*). Although you'd assume the core (the space between the skins) is empty, it's not. Instead, there are strips of corrugated cardboard, on edge, glued to the skins in an X pattern. This does a surprisingly good job of supporting the skins and prevents them from bowing in.

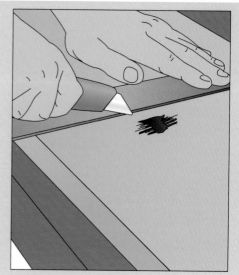

1 **Cut out the damage** To repair a hollow-core door, start by cutting out the damaged area. Although it takes a bit of elbow grease to cut through the veneer skins with a utility knife, it's the best tool for the job. I like to use a straightedge to guide the cut. This makes it easier to cut a square hole, and it's much easier to cut a patch to fit a square hole. Cut through the veneer by taking a series of light cuts. Once you've cut all four sides, remove the damaged area. If it's in one piece, set it aside to use as a pattern for the patch.

2 **Insert filler** If there is sufficient cardboard filler in the hole to support the patch, proceed to Step 3. If there isn't, cut some strips of corrugated cardboard to fit inside the door. Carefully fold the pieces along their width and insert them into the door. Unfold the pieces and position them so that they run the length of the patch. Apply a few drops of carpenter's glue where they contact the inside face of the opposite side veneer to keep them from shifting around.

3 **Make a patch** Now you can cut a patch to fit in the hole. Some home centers and hardware stores sell patch kits just for this purpose. Occasionally, you'll find a store that sells just the skins; sometimes you can purchase a damaged piece for a few dollars. If the door is painted, you can use any wood—even stiff cardboard—for the patch. Use a utility knife and a straightedge to cut the patch. Check the fit constantly and trim it as necessary.

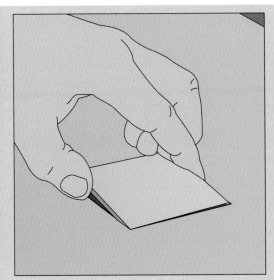

4 **Glue in the patch** All that's left is to glue in the patch. Apply a generous coat of carpenter's glue to the edges of the cardboard filler and around the edges of the hole in the veneer. Press the patch in place and secure it with masking tape or duct tape to keep it from shifting as the glue dries. Be careful not to press down too firmly, or you'll buckle the cardboard filler. When the glue dries, scrape off any excess and sand it smooth. Fill in any gaps with wood filler or putty, and apply a finish.

EXPANDING-FOAM TIP

Here's a quick way to fill the cavity inside a door to support a patch. Just give the hole a squirt of expanding foam (the minimum-expansion kind); *see the photo at right.* (Make sure to wear disposable gloves whenever you work with this stuff—it's really sticky and is tough to get off of skin.) After the foam has dried, chisel off or trim away any foam that protrudes from the hole, and then proceed with Steps 3 and 4 *described above.*

Glossary

Aluminum-clad window – a wood window where the exposed parts are covered, or clad, with aluminum.

Apron – a horizontal trim piece that fits under a windowsill.

Awning window – a type of window that is hinged on the top and swings open on the bottom.

Balance spring – a device that's used to counterbalance a sash; found in newer double-hung windows.

Balloon framing – in a balloon-framed structure, the wall studs run unbroken from sill to top plate, no matter how many stories the structure has.

Bay window – a window that projects out from a wall, typically made up of three glass panels joined at an angle.

Bi-fold door – a segmented, hinged door that slides on an overhead track and folds into itself.

Bow window – a rounded bay window that projects from a wall in a graceful arc.

Brick molding – milled wood trim piece that covers the gap between a window or door frame and the exterior wall or covering; also called brick mold.

Café door – a single or double door hung in the middle of a doorway and that swings in and out for entry.

Casement window – a window that's hinged on the side and that opens and closes via a device called a casement mechanism.

Casing – pieces of wood that are surfaced or molded on all four sides attached to the doorjamb or window jamb to cover the gap between the jamb and the wall covering.

Combination door – a door where the bottom half is wood and the top half is a screen; also called a ventilating door.

Combination window – a window assembly consisting of a half screen and two glass storm panels.

Composite door panel – a door panel made of a material other than solid wood.

Core – the center portion of a door; it may be solid wood or particleboard, and be filled with insulation or be hollow.

Cripple studs – short vertical studs installed between a header and a top plate or between the bottom of a rough sill and the sole plate.

Crossbuck – a type of door where the panels are separated by diagonal rails.

Decorative entry system – an entryway consisting of a framed door, one or two sidelights, and a transom.

Door frame – the wood parts that are assembled to form the door enclosure.

Door skin – a panel (typically wood veneer) that forms the face of a flush door.

Door trim – wood molding that's used to finish or "trim" the side of a door frame.

Double glazing – two panes of glass separated by an insulating air space, which is often filled with gas to enhance the insulating properties.

Double-hung window – a window where both the top and bottom sash can be moved.

Drip cap – a horizontal molding used to divert water from the top casing.

Entrance door – the door in the front or main entrance of a home.

Exterior casing – an exterior casing that serves as the boundary molding for the siding; often referred to as brick molding.

Fenestration – the placement or arrangement and sizing of windows in a home.

Fire-rated door – a door that's rated as to how long it will take to burn; often required between a home and an attached garage.

Flush door – any door that's made up of a core, cross-banding, and flat-face veneers.

French door – a door consisting of a top and bottom rail divided by glass panels.

Glazing – the installation of glass in a window opening.

Gliding door – a door that you open and close by sliding one or both panels along a horizontal track.

Header – a horizontal framing member that runs above rough openings to take on the load that would have been carried by the wall studs; may be solid wood, built up from 2-by material, or an engineered beam such as MicroLam or GlueLam.

Head jamb – all of the horizontal members at the top of a window or door frame.

Hollow-core door – a flush door that uses strips of carboard or other material on edge to support the face veneers.

Insulating glass – double or triple glazing with an enclosed, dehydrated, and sealed space between the panes.

Jack stud – a stud that runs between the sole plate and the bottom of the header; also referred to as a trimmer stud.

Jalousie – a type of window that's made up of glass slats that pivot open and closed.

Jamb – a vertical member at the side of a window or door frame.

Kick plate – a thin, metal plate attached to the bottom of a door to protect it from dents, scratches, and dirt.

King stud – the wall stud to which the jack stud is attached to create a rough opening for a window or door.

Load-bearing wall – a load-bearing wall helps support the weight of a house; all of the exterior walls that run perpendicular to the floor and ceiling joists in a structure are load-bearing walls, and any interior wall that's located directly above a girder or interior foundation wall is load-bearing.

Mullion – a vertical member between window units.

Muntin – a secondary framing member that's used to hold the windowpanes in a sash.

Non-load-bearing wall – a non-load-bearing wall doesn't help support the weight of the structure; also referred to as partition walls, they have relaxed design parameters and code requirements such as wider stud spacing (24" vs. 16" on-center) and smaller headers.

Panel door – a door made up of panels that fit in a frame consisting of stiles and rails.

Parting strip – a thin wood strip that separates the upper sash and lower sash into two channels so that they can slide up and down independently.

Patio door – a door that opens onto a patio or deck; usually made of glass to allow viewing.

Platform framing – a platform-framed structure is built one story at a time; each story is built upon a platform that consists of joists and a subfloor.

Rail – a cross or horizontal portion of a frame.

Raised door panel – a door panel where the edges are shaped to give the panel the appearance of being "raised" above the frame.

Replacement window – typically a double-hung window that's bought as a kit to replace a window without disturbing the interior or exterior walls.

Rough opening – an opening that's sized to accept a window or door; a horizontal framing member called a header is installed to assume the load of the wall studs that were removed; the header is supported by jack studs that are attached to full-length wall studs.

Rough sill – a horizontal framing member that defines the bottom of a window's rough opening.

Sash – a framework of rails and stiles that holds the panes of a window.

Sash door – a door where the bottom half is made of wood and the top is made of glass.

Shim – a thin piece of wood that, when driven behind a surface, forces it to become level or plumb.

Sidelight – an assembly of stiles and rails and glass panels that are attached to one or both sides of an exterior door.

Sill – the main horizontal member forming the bottom of the door frame.

Single-hung window – a window similar to a double-hung, where only the bottom sash moves up and down.

Stile – an upright or vertical part of a frame.

Stool – the piece of window trim that provides a stop for the lower sash and extends the sill into the room.

Storm door – any door that covers and protects an exterior door.

Temporary supports – temporary supports bear the weight that a wall normally would, until a new support system can be installed (such as a new header or beam).

Threshold – a wood or metal strip attached to the bottom of a door to cover the gap between the sill and the floor.

Transom – a horizontal member separating one window panel from another; or a small window installed above a door and typically hinged at the bottom to provide ventilation.

Index